Havana

Following the crisis of the Special Period, Cuba promoted urban agriculture throughout its towns and cities to address food sovereignty and security. Through the adoption of state recommended design strategies, these gardens have become places of social and economic exchange throughout Cuba. This book maps the lived experiences surrounding three urban farms in Havana to construct a deeper understanding about the everyday life of this city. Using narratives and drawings, this research uncovers these sites as places where education, intimacy, entrepreneurism, wellbeing, and culture are interwoven alongside food production. Henri Lefebvre's latent work on rhythmanalysis is used as a research method to capture the everyday beats particular to Havana surrounding these sites. This book maps the many ways in which these spaces shift power away from the state to become places that are co-created by the community to serve as a crucial hinge point between the ongoing collapse of the city and its future wellbeing.

Susan Anne Mansel Fitzgerald, PhD is the Design Director and Managing Partner at FBM. She is also an Assistant Professor at Dalhousie University Faculty of Architecture and Planning. She lives in Halifax, Nova Scotia, Canada.

T0347740

Built Environment City Studies

The *Built Environment City Studies* series provides researchers and academics with a detailed look at individual cities through a specific lens. These concise books delve into a case study of an international city, focusing on a key built environment topic. Written by scholars from around the world, the collection provides a library of thorough studies into trends, developments and approaches that affect our cities.

Rio de Janeiro
Urban Expansion and Environment
José L. S. Gámez, Zhongjie Lin and Jeffrey S Nesbit

Kuala Lumpur
Community, Infrastructure and Urban Inclusivity
Marek Kozłowski, Asma Mehan and Krzysztof Nawratek

Glasgow
High-Rise Homes, Estates and Communities in the Post-War Period
Lynn Abrams, Ade Kearns, Barry Hazley and Valerie Wright

Pemba
Spontaneous Living Spaces
Corinna Del Bianco

Vienna
Still a Just City?
Edited by Yuri Kazepov and Roland Verwiebe

For more information about this series, please visit: www.routledge.com/
Built-Environment-City-Studies/book-series/BECS

Havana

Mapping Lived Experiences of Urban Agriculture

Susan Anne Mansel Fitzgerald

NEW YORK AND LONDON

First published 2022
by Routledge
605 Third Avenue, New York, NY 10158

and by Routledge
4 Park Square, Milton Park, Abingdon, Oxon OX14 4RN

Routledge is an imprint of the Taylor & Francis Group, an informa business

British Library Cataloguing-in-Publication Data
A catalogue record for this book is available from the British Library

Library of Congress Cataloging-in-Publication Data
Names: Fitzgerald, Susan Anne Mansel, author.
Title: Havana : mapping lived experiences of urban agriculture /
    Susan Anne Mansel Fitzgerald.
Description: Abingdon, Oxon ; New York, NY : Routledge, 2022. |
    Series: Built environment city studies | Includes bibliographical
    references and index.
Identifiers: LCCN 2022007069 (print) | LCCN 2022007070 (ebook) |
    ISBN 9781032062556 (hardback) | ISBN 9781032062563 (paperback) |
    ISBN 9781003201410 (ebook)
Subjects: LCSH: Urban agriculture—Cuba—History. | Food sovereignty—
    Cuba—History.
Classification: LCC S477.C9 F58 2022 (print) | LCC S477.C9 (ebook) |
    DDC 635.9/77097291—dc23/eng/20220316
LC record available at https://lccn.loc.gov/2022007069
LC ebook record available at https://lccn.loc.gov/2022007070

ISBN: 978-1-032-06255-6 (hbk)
ISBN: 978-1-032-06256-3 (pbk)
ISBN: 978-1-003-20141-0 (ebk)

DOI: 10.4324/9781003201410

Typeset in Times New Roman
by Apex CoVantage, LLC

To Brainard, Will, and Sophie Fitzgerald for helping me see the world differently—each in your own particular way—and for your enduring love.

Contents

Illustrations

Acknowledgements

Thank you to:

Professor Peter Bishop and Professor Iain Borden at the Bartlett, UCL for your guidance, patience, and insight throughout the original PhD.

The professors and students from Universidad Tecnológica de La Habana José Antonio Echeverría (CUJAE). Particular thanks go to Professor Jorge Peña Díaz, Professor Joiselen Cazanave Macías, and Fernando Martirena Cordovés. None of this work would have been possible without your dedicated help and friendship over many years.

The students and faculty from Dalhousie University School of Architecture who travelled with me to Cuba and shared in the research over the years.

Stavros Kondeas, Rita Wang, Alicia McDowell (Gilmore), and Lucas McDowell for all your help producing the artwork.

My mother, Dr. Margaret Porter, for your love, kindness, and support over many years.

Brainard Fitzgerald for being by my side and part of the study every step of the way.

1 Introduction

1.1 Urban Agriculture in Havana

Food shapes a place and there is a direct relationship between cities and the sustenance they provide to their inhabitants. How a city procures, produces, and distributes food is an everchanging interplay of its people, processes, and places. Agriculture has historically been part of civic life, with garden plots and the pasturing of animals occurring within the communal commons of cities and towns. To reflect this connection, the word 'agriculture' is derived from the Latin words *agri* meaning field and *colere* which denotes caring or cultivation. The original idea of farming was as much about tending the earth as it was about advancing an idea, or the collective identity or culture of a place.[1] With industrial agriculture, this connection no longer exists as the production of food is separated from the point of consumption and, in doing so, it has also moved away from the original definition of the word. However, care and growing still exist alongside one another within urban farms as they continue to create deep connections between people, production, and specific places.

People engage with urban agriculture for various reasons. Some participate in it as a hobby, enjoying the visceral connection to nature through this social and ecological activity. Communities are often concerned with the authenticity of their food and a local garden empowers this connection. Lastly and perhaps most importantly, those facing extreme hardship grow food close to where they live to feed their families and to keep starvation at bay. The last reason on the list mobilised urban agriculture in Cuba. However, the deployment was not only developed by desperate and hungry citizens but it was also actively organised by the government both nationally and locally. Since the Special Period of the 1990s this movement has evolved to become much more than the human desire for food sovereignty and security but rather it is linked to the original definition of 'agriculture'—involving care and culture—bolstered by broad community efforts. So, while these sites of urban agriculture might be considered an

DOI: 10.4324/9781003201410-1

unusual research area for an architect who is interested in studying Havana, Cuba, it was the co-creation of these cultivated spaces throughout this palimpsestic city that piqued my curiosity as to how one might re-consider the possibilities of urban space and question how these sites might 'act as generators—or, more precisely, as re-generators' of this collapsing city.[2]

Urban agricultural gardens are located within all of the municipalities and neighbourhoods of Havana (Figure 1.2) and, in contrast to the city's declining built environments, these sites of urban food production have been successfully implemented through seamless cultivation-to-community connections. The study is particularly interesting as these productive sites are embedded into all of the social and political tiers of the country and the community. These gardens exist in-between the triumph of the Revolution that promised equal access to provisions and healthcare and the everyday realities surrounding the scarcity of food and medicine. The sites are dependent upon the resourcefulness of the workers, the demands and preferences of local consumers, access to infrastructure, and the realities of the surrounding context. Influenced by global, seasonal, and everyday rhythms, these spaces represent a paradigm shift from a state supply of food to local self-sufficient provisioning within the emerging Cuban entrepreneurial economic model. Involving spatial tactics of appropriation and negotiation, these gardens are simultaneously places for pleasure, celebration, and survival. And ultimately, these gardens are full of the 'subversive potential of urban spaces' as they offer an understanding that the world must not only be interpreted but is always changing, just as it had done during and after the Revolution.[3]

So how should one go about unpacking the tangle of people and places surrounding these gardens within the city to reveal their characteristics? It is clear that '[t]he supply of food to a great city is one of the most remarkable of social phenomena' so studying such spaces will disclose much about the place, especially since the preparation, production, and consumption of food within cities each have their own intrinsic rhythms.[4] These rhythms are grounded within everyday life and embrace domesticity, employment, provisioning, education, healthcare, and ecology, and so it would seem important to uncover the beats of quotidian activities surrounding these sites. Taking this as a direction, this book adopts a conceptual framework surrounding the study of site-specific everyday rhythms based upon Henri Lefebvre's incipient work on rhythmanalysis, to study the city. These beats are not understood as scientific but as atmospheric, process, people, and place dependent.

1.2   Research Questions

The research draws on the work of Lefebvre to question how sites of agriculture within communities affect urban life in Havana, not by serving as a

1. La Sazón, *Nuevo Vedado, Plaza de la Revolución*

2. Alto Rendimiento, *Cayo Hueso, Centro Habana*

3. Huerto Intensivo, *San Isidro, La Habana Vieja*

Figure 1.1 Sites of urban agriculture

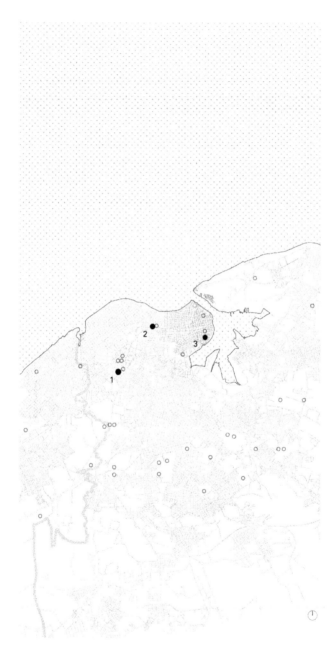

Figure 1.2 Map of Havana showing sites of urban agriculture visited throughout the province

neutral backdrop for food production but rather as enabling a deeper understanding of the city: spatially, socially, economically, and ecologically. It focuses on people and how they participate in everyday life. The quotidian activities that surround these sites render an understanding of the city as being 'ordinary'. For Amin and Graham, this idea of ordinary encompassed everyday life and the political, economic, and social layers that contributed to the specific experiences of the city.[5] Jennifer Robinson used the term ordinary to describe cities, as opposed to categories such as Western or third world, developed or underdeveloped, global north or global south, as she believed these other terms suggested an understanding of a city that is striving to develop into something else and somehow does not feel that it is modern—and so her use of the term 'ordinary' meets the city where it is at.[6] Either of the two definitions of the word ordinary support a study that encompasses the quotidian life of the city of Havana. This is an important moment to capture as the city of Havana hovers at the point of multiple possibilities and paradoxes, including socialism or capitalism; collapse or development; scarcity or abundance; and global isolation or integration.

The research considers the following questions within different sites of urban agriculture and their surrounding community:

1. What spatial practices and patterns (rhythms) are demonstrated in and around sites of urban agriculture?
2. How do sites of urban agriculture affect their surrounding neighbourhoods?
3. Do these urban gardens contribute to the resilience of the city?[7]
4. What can we learn about urban development from these sites?

This research believes that urban agriculture in Havana enables positive change, that these gardens enhance the lived condition of their communities and that this, in turn, improves the city socially, economically, and ecologically in addition to providing food security and sovereignty. These spaces are performative and sensorial; the activities within and around them, the smells, colours, and textures improve the urban realm.[8] With this in mind, this study documents the spatial practices and patterns of these sites to understand their impact within communities in Havana.

1.3 Using Henri Lefebvre as a Guide

Architects and planners have readily absorbed Lefebvre's work on the *Production of Space* without necessarily linking it to his larger body of work involving the *Critique of Everyday Life* or *Rhythmanalysis: Space, Time and Everyday Life*; in each of these he proposed analysing urban rhythms. The *Production of Space* asserts that space is a social product that is composed of overlapping and contradictory criteria that change over time. These modifications are due to the specificity of the urban context and the activities that occur within and around the space, the conscious ideas that designers used to create it, and the experiences and encounters that occur within it. Rhythmanalysis gives us a methodology with which to study this concept dialectically by helping us to understand the multiple rhythms of these sites and how they intersect with the everyday life of the city to create a collective *oeuvre*.[9] The overarching strategies for looking at these sites in the city are derived from Iain Borden's *Skateboarding, Space and the City: Architecture and the Body*; and Stuart Elden, Elizabeth Lebas, and Eleonore Kofman's *Henri Lefebvre*, and include the principles discussed in the following sections.

1.3.1 Encounter

This study involves participation. Just as Lefebvre's studies involved going 'into the field' and partaking 'in real life' so this work engages with the sites of urban agriculture with an understanding that in order to get to know something one must in some small way interact with it.[10] Perspectives from inside and outside the space are mutually important in *The Production of Space*, as Lefebvre considered concurrent encounters and interconnections between the perceived, the conceived, and the lived dimensions of space. Multiple actors shape these urban agricultural sites, including the state, the planners, the producers, the community, and the consumers, all within the physical realities and contexts of the different sites. These relationships are not static but in constant flux, such that one could think of them as on-going re-productions of space. An encounter with a site of urban agriculture requires studying a site in multiple ways:

1. Spatial practice or perceived space. This is the study of the physical or material aspects of a site and includes characteristics such as the morphology, typology, topography, and flow of materials into and out of the garden; the 'production of material goods'.[11]
2. Representations of space or conceived space. This includes the rules surrounding the creation of sites as outlined in the official standards on urban agriculture and documented in city by-laws and codes. It includes the designs of these gardens by architects, planners, and landscape architects; the 'production of knowledge'.[12]
3. Spaces of representation or lived space. This is the study of the actual uses and alternative representations of these sites and any 'clandestine' practices.[13] These gardens are activated and given new meaning

through social activity and the imagination; this leads to the 'production of meaning'.[14,15]

Each of these categories has its own rhythms.[16] Studying all of these beats certainly does not make the city legible but rather provides a mechanism with which to start to see its illegibility, to talk about it intelligibly, and to use these as tools with which to consider the future city.

1.3.2 The Right to the City

Lefebvre's writing stressed the need for citizens to have some control of their city and the need to shift power away from the state and towards urban inhabitants through the act of co-creation. Most cities value space for its 'exchange value' rather than its 'use value'. Private property and the market are prioritised over the collective space. This is not the case in Cuba and many aspects of Cuban life occur in shared spaces. The narrow streets are continually arranged and rearranged as beer cans mark out the corners of a soccer pitch or baseball field; tools on a road define a workshop for bicycle or car repair; for gym class at a primary school, a rope is stretched across the end of a road to prohibit vehicular access; and an assortment of chairs are brought into a street to form a living room where people catch up on the daily gossip.[17]

1.3.3 Everyday Life

According to John Chase and others, everyday space is 'the connective tissue that binds daily lives together'.[18] Lefebvre focused on everyday life and its various rhythms, believing that an understanding of the various manifestations of space over time was the key to comprehending complex sociospatial interrelationships. Havana is a city where much within the everyday is a struggle, including commuting to work on crowded old buses, insecure food supply, collapsing buildings, and frequent water and power outages. All of these challenges create conflicting rhythms within this city of everyday lived complexity. '*No es fácil*' (it is not easy) and '*Es complicado*' (it is complicated) are two common Cuban expressions. Multiple economies further confuse the situation where residents must constantly extemporise to survive.

> [I]nventar is commonly used in Cuban vernacular speech to describe processes of improvising creative solutions to everyday problems.[19]

Lefebvre characterises everyday life as a territory of conflict between cyclical and linear time. In Cuba, *la lucha* (the fight) is a term commonly used to describe this daily struggle. Life encompasses multiple everyday difficulties imposed through linear time involving intermittent access to infrastructure and commodities and being subjected to the bureaucracy and inefficiencies of the government—all of these have their own specific rhythms. Together with cyclical time, they define the character that surrounds sites of urban agriculture, and their polyrhythmic nature tells us much about everyday life within Havana.

1.3.4 The Body

The relationship of urban agriculture and the body are realised through the actual physical work of cultivation, the consumption of the harvest for food and homeopathic medicine, and the celebrations and religious practices in which these plants are used. Bringing together these cultural and biological rhythms is at the core of rhythmanalysis.

In urban agriculture, the body works hard and humans perform the work of machines that are normally associated with industrial farming. While the body toils within a garden in the city, it is detached from the urban experience. As the senses of smell, taste, and touch engage with the plants and nature, the body and mind escape from the overcrowded and deteriorating city to a place that grows and flourishes.

The apparatus of the Cuban state is responsible for maintaining healthy bodies and this is a device for measuring its success both locally and globally. The government employs an impressive number of health professionals throughout multiple neighbourhood programmes. At a community level, this involves teams of physicians and nurses who are located within clinics called *consultorios del médico de la familia*. Each clinic serves approximately 120 families or from 600 to 700 persons. In Havana, these clinics are organised on most city blocks, with the nurse and doctor living alongside the community.[20] Healthcare transpires through close proximity to the community through everyday observation that includes preventative strategies, education, and rehabilitation, as much as responding to a health crisis. With severe shortages of pharmaceutical drugs and the most basic medical supplies, practitioners have few options other than to procure medicine from alternative sources and treatments. Such medical techniques, called traditional, natural, or green medicine, are encouraged by the government and taught alongside biomedicine in medical schools. Pharmacies carry a greater selection of these alternative medicines than they do allopathic treatments, especially for everyday ailments. Medicinal gardens are sometimes located close to the *consultorios* and occasionally the doctors and nurses are responsible for the cultivation of the plants they prescribe.

1.4 Research Method

Against this background of scarcity, the slow decay of infrastructure and the sudden collapse of buildings, the resourcefulness of everyday invention thrives in a city that continually adapts through everyday life.[21] It is impossible to construct an intelligible, rational city from this informality, but it is easy to identify the urban rhythms that involve 'particularities and similarities, repetition and difference, rupture and continuities'.[22] While this is not strictly scientific, rhythmanalysis certainly gives us an understanding of what is most ubiquitous, vivid, and important in everyday life.[23] Rhythmanalysis is composed of cyclical time that encompasses seasons, circadian rhythms, and life cycles. It also consists of linear time that involves timetables that are regulated by the clock, such as work, allocated breaks, and schedules. Studying these multiple and simultaneous rhythms within the sites of cultivation that are embedded within a community reveals contradictions and connections that exist between production and consumption, and society and the state.

Lefebvre is less clear about how to pursue this study, although we know that the rhythmanalyst has to be both part of it and exterior to it, with the suggestion of observing from a distance, such as from a balcony, to allow for analysis.[24] These different perspectives include participation and interpretation—making rhythmanalysis a dialectical study that is not strictly scientific but rather atmospheric, people and place dependent.[25]

1.4.1 Case Study Selection

This study involved fieldwork that took place at three case study sites in Havana (Figures 1.1, 1.2, and 1.4). The selection of the sites focused on three different municipalities within the city's Central Zone (Figure 1.3). Each site is highly typo-morphological within its specific neighbourhood, meaning that the sites are representative of the broader surrounding context—although certainly not characteristic of the whole city. Havana is a poly-centric city, and each community was produced during a different epoch. The Laws of the Indies imposed by the Spanish were generally applied to the original colonial centre, La Habana Vieja, with its plazas, narrow streets, and grid pattern. San Isidro is the community to the south of La Habana Vieja. The specific site occupies a space where a house collapsed around 1990. The second site is in Centro Habana. This place emerged in the nineteenth century after the demolition of the city's wall, so as to accommodate the expanding city population. In the early twentieth century, the USA invested in the suburbs to the west of the centre, in the Vedado and Miramar neighbourhoods (in the municipalities of Playa and Plaza de la

Revolución) through the creation of parks and vegetated streets. This meant that Centro Habana was left to the Afro-Cubans and low-income residents and the municipality's buildings now have the highest rates of decay and most compromised infrastructure in the country. Cayo Hueso, within Centro Habana, is emblematic of this, with much of its housing stock in very bad condition. The third site, Plaza de la Revolución, is eclectic with its high, mid-rise, and multi-unit residential housing complexes that surround the civic and political heart of the city. Home to many sites of urban agriculture, the *organopónico* (urban farm) that was selected for this study is on land deemed too wet for the development of housing.

Certain sites within each municipality were contemplated, tested, and then later rejected, as they were too unique and their context within the city was not representative of the typo-morphology of their neighbourhoods. Others did not engage with the societal activities that took place at their boundaries, if they were, for example, surrounded by roads with heavy traffic. All of these selected sites are polyrhythmic and proto-typical. The urban stories they tell are representative of the communities in which they exist. In aggregate, they offer a glimpse into the different spatial, social, and temporal urban typo-morphological conditions that exist within the city of Havana.

Central Zone
Intermediate Zone
Peripheral Zone

1 Playa	6 La Habana del Este	11 Marianao
2 Plaza de la Revolución	7 Guanabacoa	12 La Lisa
3 Centro Habana	8 San Miguel del Padrón	13 Boyeros
4 La Habana Vieja	9 Diez de Octubre	14 Arroyo Naranjo
5 Regla	10 Cerro	15 Cotorro

Figure 1.3 Location of the municipalities in Havana

Figure 1.4 Location of the three study communities within Havana

1.4.2 Methodology

The research methodology involved both far and near study, including participant observation, semi-structured interviews, and spatial analysis. This type of observation involved recording the activities, atmospheres, and urban rhythms that surrounded the sites, including identifiable categories such as socialising or purchasing provisions. These events took place within the streets and the observations were made by being close to the gardens so as to observe everyday activities and record them by making drawings and notes or taking photographs and videos.

To facilitate participant observation on the sites, I organised a master's level design studio, taking students from Dalhousie University School of Architecture, Halifax, Canada, to study the sites of urban food production in conjunction with students and faculty from the School of Architecture at the Universidad Tecnológica de La Habana José Antonio Echeverría (CUJAE) in Havana. This class involved both formal and informal visits to the sites of production and meetings with administrative organisations. Having Cuban students and faculty from within the communities engaged in the work enabled collaboration with and trust from the inhabitants of the

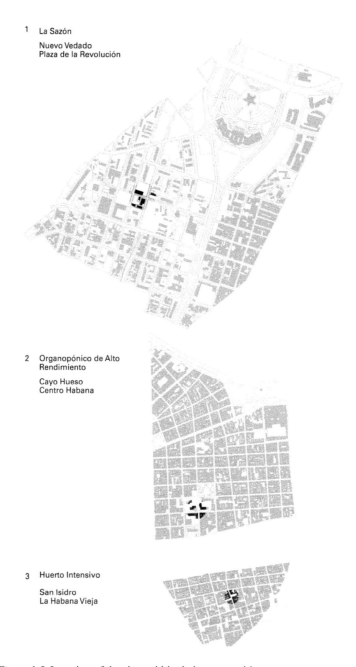

1 La Sazón

Nuevo Vedado
Plaza de la Revolución

2 Organopónico de Alto
Rendimiento

Cayo Hueso
Centro Habana

3 Huerto Intensivo

San Isidro
La Habana Vieja

Figure 1.5 Location of the sites within their communities

neighbourhood. It also contextualised the spaces within the surrounding community and was invaluable for Spanish-to-English translation. The food producers on the sites understood that the research was concerned with the everyday activities that took place within the garden and surrounding the sites. As this research studio had been on-going for multiple years (2014–2019), the producers and people in the surrounding community recognised and welcomed us (Dalhousie University students with me and the professors from CUJAE with their students). We involved them in the discussions and shared the drawings and photographs with them each year.

During the first visit, the students and I conducted semi-structured interviews with the head producer. Here we posed questions to gain some background information. This information also served to verify the observations made inside and outside the gardens and to show distinctions between what people said and what they actually did. Research visas for this study were obtained from CUJAE, as the Cuban government does not authorise research within Cuba without explicit permission. However, spearheading an academic programme with student learning opportunities was encouraged and supported.

1.5 Recording the Rhythms

Lefebvre gave no exact method for recording urban rhythms other than 'memory' so there was a need to develop a recording device to document the discovered patterns of the city that moved between the qualitative and the quantitative, the lived and the analytical.[26] Many have used words and film as the media to document rhythms.[27] Lefebvre conducted several studies of architecture and urban spaces with the Institut de Sociologie Urbaine (ISU), including one in which he assessed why people favoured detached housing with gardens, over collective housing. The methods of research involved the coding of interview responses to obtain quantitative data. Lefebvre believed that these interviews instigated defence mechanisms among the occupants and that the data was flawed.[28,29] So instead, he favoured the approach of his student Philippe Boudon who documented spaces using drawings and photographs to show the evolving transformations people made to the houses, which were originally designed by Le Corbusier, to reveal the occupants' spatial practices and preferences over time. Likewise, my work as an architect led me to a qualitative analysis of these sites through drawings that depict spaces, atmospheres, and experiences as both analytical and illustrative tools. Drawings are used in this study as an instrument for both finding out and revealing how space is iteratively produced and reproduced. This involved drawing and mapping the specificity of a site, the local networks of its citizens and the surrounding urban context. This study was initially done by referencing existing Autocad plans and the very minimally available geographic information system (GIS) data on Havana. It also involved obtaining information on the individual buildings from the National Archives of Cuba located in Havana, taking site measurements, and drawing the context. Completed over six years, this type of work did not homogenise the city but rather detected its changing rhythms so as to uncover the city's possibilities.[30] Unlike the media of film or text, these drawings depicted the precise qualities of the spaces, including the adjacencies, the dimensions, the hidden moments, and the changes over time. Within the plans and the sections, different rhythms came into view which exposed the lived experience of urban space surrounding these gardens.[31]

1.6 Everyday Rhythms Particular to Havana

Rhythmanalysis involves time. In the context of Havana, it focuses on the quotidian goings on that surround sites of urban agriculture, including the hours of operation and the groups that gather; the commuters passing by and engaging with the space; the school children visiting for lessons on cultivation; the elderly or unwell buying their medications; the Santería practitioners looking for plants to use for specific rituals; the lonely and underemployed watching the site; the different transactions and economies surrounding the garden; inspections by government administrators; the heat of the day and the afternoon downpours; the preparation for and havoc of hurricanes; the workday chores and seasonal changes; the intermittent schedule of electricity and water supply; the untimely collapse of structures, both on the site and involving the surrounding buildings; repair and maintenance schedules; the community mosquito fumigation programmes; and the neighbourhood events and festivals. Associated with all these rhythms are six sub-narratives that pervade all aspects of Cuban life: *inventar*, living amongst the ruins, the complexities of the Cuban economy, the evolving ideas surrounding the Revolution, Afro-Cuban religions, and *los socios*. Each of these categories are rhythmic as they produce and reproduce the physical environment over time.

> Everywhere where there is interaction between a place, a time and an expenditure of energy, there is a rhythm.[32]

1.6.1 Inventar

In 1992, Editora Verde Olivo, the publishing house of the Cuban Revolutionary Armed Forces, released *Con Nuestros Propios Esfuerzos: Algunas Experiencias para Enfrentar el Período Especial en Tiempo de Paz* (With Our Own Efforts: Some Experiences to Confront the Special Period in Time of Peace). This book documented survival strategies that were employed during the Special Period. These involved tips on growing food, recipes using alternative ingredients, and strategies for repairing domestic devices. While the book was circulated by the state, Cuba's resourcefulness came from its citizens. This change from state control to individual ingenuity signified a huge departure in communist Cuba as the government relinquished power and the practices of *bricolage* and *inventar* thrived.[33]

Everyday life in the Western world is defined by forced consumption and built-in obsolescence. *Inventar*, on the other hand, has very different rhythms as it includes the requirement for daily social interactions. This includes the sourcing of materials and products within multiple economies, reimagining uses for items so that everything is recycled, and negotiating political and community relationships to make necessary acquisitions.[34] Valuing "use value" as opposed to "exchange value" with its associated protection of personal property means that projects are less fixed in space as *inventar* flows and expands across boundaries, throughout the community, fuelled by negotiation and invention.

1.6.2 Living Amongst the Ruins

> By spring of 2008, there were one to three partial or complete collapses a day in the entire city. Partial building collapses range from part of a balcony breaking off to a roof or wall falling down.[35]

Buildings continually collapse in Havana (Figure 1.6) and all that is solid turns to dust as the land a house once occupied reverts to the government. The timelines and rhythms of this phenomenon are important. They often involve repeated warnings by authorities to vacate dangerous buildings and many attempts to prop up buildings at risk of collapse. Once buildings have fully or partially collapsed, emergency services arrive to triage the dead and injured and the occupants are relocated. If they decide to stay in their damaged home, they are forced to contract their dwelling space into the remaining salvageable area. The community grieves for its lost neighbours while care facilities are found for the injured and shelters for the dispossessed. After this relocation, the site is scavenged for useful building materials. Over time the authorities may clear the debris and secure the site against trespassers and eventually there may emerge a transient use for the land involving storage, parking, or gardening. Occasionally a new building is designed and constructed, and the previous occupants re-inhabit the new structure. This last step almost never occurs. People are often given multiple warnings to vacate decaying residences, but they frequently resist

Figure 1.6 Collapsed building

relocation, primarily because they will lose ownership of their property. Vacating is also extremely disruptive to the rhythms of people's lives as temporary shelters are typically located in the periphery of the city and these displacements are usually indefinite. If their building partially collapses, families often work around the debris and shrink their living arrangements (Figure 4.9).[36] Years of deferred maintenance means that doing nothing is not an option for Havana and in some parts of the city it is already too late to save the building stock.[37] Either way, this research understands decay and collapse as dynamic rhythms of the city of Havana and the beats are intimately linked to these gardens, as these sites are often created as a result of a localised building collapse.

1.6.3 Multiple Economies

During the study period, Cuba had several economies and circulating currencies. The two official currencies were the peso Cubano (Cuban peso or CUP) and the peso Cubano convertible (convertible peso or CUC). The CUP was the national currency, while the CUC could be exchanged for hard currencies.[38] It was also considered the currency for tourists and for Cubans who wished to purchase what might be considered luxury items, with some items being paid for in both currencies, depending on the quantity or quality. US dollars are also part of the economy and many Cubans receive regular remittances from friends and relatives overseas. Government-employed Cubans were paid in Cuban pesos and, according to Cuba's National Office of Statistics, in 2015 the official average monthly salary was 687 pesos, or about 25 CUCs ($25 US), with a professional earning 40 CUCs per month.[39] However, salaries vary considerably, with most Cubans operating between multiple economies. In fact, conversations with Cubans suggested that a living wage was closer to 100 CUCs a month, approaching 400 CUCs for what might be considered a good standard of living. Since January 2021 there is only one official currency. However, this discrepancy still exists and people compensate for the shortfall by trading hard currencies, second jobs, pilfering from places of employment, and informal activities that are initiated through friends and community relationships.

There are state stores and non-state shops from which to purchase goods (Figure 1.7). The latter is composed of surplus produce that can be lawfully sold outside of the state stores at agricultural or farmers markets (*Mercados Agropecuarios*) and points of sale (*Puntos de Venta*). The informal economy includes both the underground market and the *bolsa negra* (black market). The former involves the sale of products directly to customers or to go-betweens who mark up the prices of their commodities and then sell them at a profit. As these sales occur outside of state control, the government does not collect taxes on them. While the Cuban government does not support these

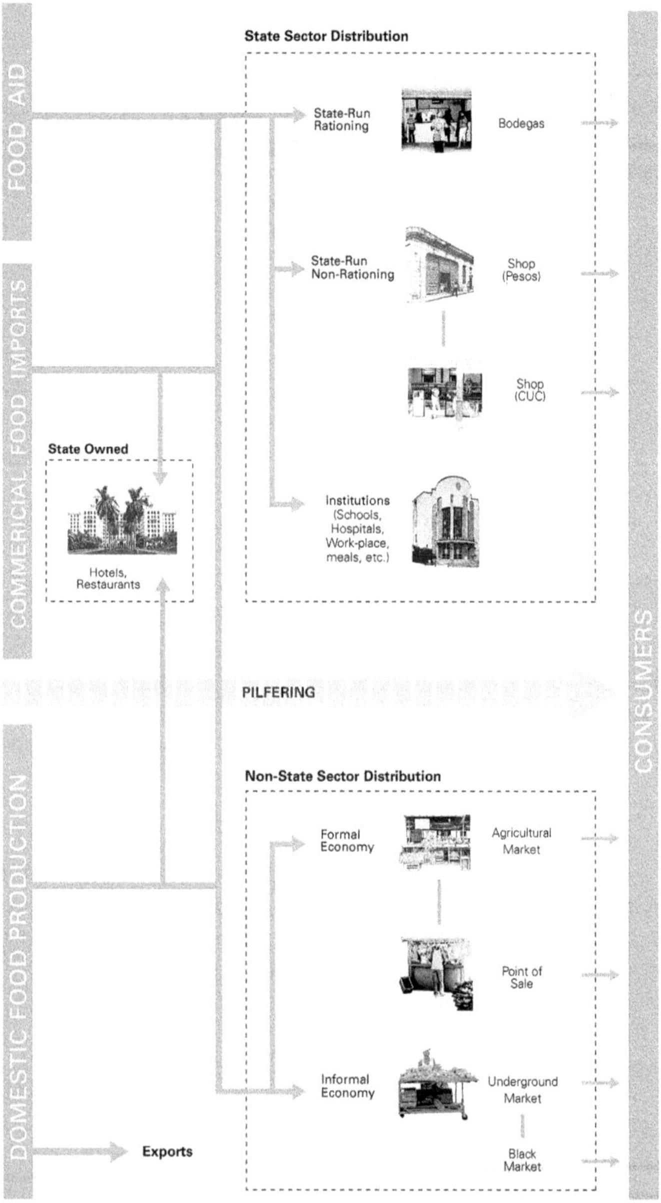

State Sector Distribution

FOOD AID

COMMERCIAL FOOD IMPORTS

State-Run Rationing — Bodegas

State-Run Non-Rationing — Shop (Pesos)

Shop (CUC)

State Owned

Hotels, Restaurants

Institutions (Schools, Hospitals, Work-place, meals, etc.)

PILFERING

CONSUMERS

Non-State Sector Distribution

DOMESTIC FOOD PRODUCTION

Formal Economy — Agricultural Market

Point of Sale

Informal Economy — Underground Market

Exports — Black Market

* Information obtained from Office of Global Analysis, FAS, USDA, Cuba's Food & Agriculture Situation Report page 19-20

Figure 1.7 Food supply chain in Cuba

underground activities, it typically does not challenge these actions as they actively facilitate people's efforts to obtain food.[40] The black market involves selling and buying goods that Cubans are prohibited from buying, such as beef—'cows are officially the property of the Cuban state . . . and no cow can be sold or eaten privately'—its illegal use can lead to incarceration.[41]

Trabajadores por cuenta propia describes self-employed workers who operate outside of the state-controlled centralised economy. This practice has been legal in Cuba since 1993 but it is limited to a list of 201 legal occupations; self-employment is, in some capacity, controversial within the Cuban economy as it signifies the emergence of individuals working for private gain.[42] Some see it as the certain demise of Cuba's socialist system and the emergence of capitalism. However, the Cuban government's strict regulations, licensing fees, and high income taxes mean the contributions the self-employed make to the state are significant. In fact, the process of self-employment is seen as so arduous that many individuals abandon the practice and return to state employment, with the ease of pilfering and the ability to access the black market. Despite all of this, the Cuban government is actively encouraging forty percent of Cubans to move towards self-employment, with the cooperative being one of the most common and encouraged forms of enterprise, as these are based on the social values of cooperatives that include 'self-help, self-responsibility, democracy, equality, equity, and solidarity'.[43] Such attributes keep the cooperative ideology in line with the Cuban government's ideas of entrepreneurship. Sites of urban agriculture have always existed within multiple market sectors. Often run as cooperatives, they are part of a complex network of economies and ecologies within the community and are quite different from the bureaucracy of the state.[44]

1.6.4 La Revolución versus Revolution

Cuba is defined by La Revolución, the 1959 seizing of power. However, the word 'revolution' has multiple temporal definitions. While it is often used to describe an abrupt change in power, the word also describes a cyclical event.[45] The complexity of the use of the word in the Cuban context is important as revolution is an evolving concept and both definitions apply especially to a study that involves the investigation of rhythms.

Lefebvre's theories about urbanisation are all-encompassing and revolutionary while also being quotidian. Likewise, the Revolution in Cuba was about a complete confrontation that overthrew the authoritarian government of the Cuban president Fulgencio Batista.[46] Initially rooted entirely within the present, the Revolution was about the heroic sacrifice of the country's young, dynamic leaders. However, this event is also positioned as a much longer struggle that involved colonialisation and the past wars of independence against Spain. Suffice it is to say that the revolution in Cuba is 'constantly changing' and this manifests through evolving everyday life.[47] Cuba continually re-evaluates itself, having survived multiple setbacks and criticisms: in 1962–1963, the economic crisis threatened to upset the new government; in 1970, a ten million ton sugar harvest (*zafra*) failed; in 1989, the Soviet Bloc collapsed and the associated countries adopted capitalism; in 2007, a nationwide participatory consultation sought out the public criticisms that were found to be rampant throughout the entire system.[48] Over sixty years on, the Revolution encompasses all aspects of Cuban life, including its urban realm and the everyday life of the individual—so much so that, in everyday conversation, people refer to themselves as 'good revolutionaries'. The values of the Revolution included free education and healthcare, and accessible food and housing. These social ambitions have been hard to meet, and each has had to be reconsidered in multiple ways. However, as Marina Gold notes, the gardens subscribe to the principles of the Revolution through ecology and entrepreneurialism within a social and altruistic context, such that they could be thought of as revolutionary spaces.[49]

> A revolution that does not produce a new space has not realised its full potential.[50]

1.6.5 Socialismo versus Sociolismo

This concept of *socialismo* versus *sociolismo* involves understanding that much of Cuban life is shaped by social relationships rather than by state ideology or by being a *socialista* (socialist). In a country where it is difficult to procure even the most basic necessities, *sociolismo* (a play on the word for socialism) is 'the unofficial network of people satisfying [their] needs through partnerships' where the word '*socio* means business partner'.[51] People are essential to any kind of negotiation in Cuba, from lending a hand, to watching out for someone, to chipping in, or keeping an ear to the ground as to who needs or wants certain services or goods.

> They call it *sociolismo*, an invented word that roughly translated means the buddy system. It refers to the network of friends and relatives that Cubans use to pierce through bureaucracy, cope with chronic shortages and resolve everyday problems. In cash-poor Cuba, connections are as good as currency.[52]

Each endeavour requires the reciprocal exchange of favours by a network of contacts, friends, or acquaintances. Exhausting at times, the rhythms of these partnerships involve conviviality, creativity, and collaboration so as to circumvent bureaucratic restrictions to obtain certain goods. Mainly done without reliable access to the internet, *sociolismo* is visceral and time dependent. Favours and generosity are remembered as credit for future transactions. Reliability and discretion form a type of currency. All of this contributes to the everyday re-distribution of goods and services. Sites of urban agriculture serve as hubs for these exchanges of favours.

1.6.6 Santería Practices

Santería is a syncretic religion that was derived from Yoruba beliefs and some Roman Catholic ideology that spread by word of mouth. It is a pragmatic religion that focuses on everyday activities particularly the maintenance of wellbeing. Centred around maintaining relationships with the mortal saints, or *orishas*, the Santería religion involves offerings and sacrifices that aim to keep the *orishas* satisfied. This religion has increased in popularity due to the scarcities that were inherent during the Special Period, as it is believed that the *orishas* offer practical assistance if practitioners carry out the appropriate rituals. Followers believe that making regular sacrifices and propitiations to the saints will help them achieve their preordained destiny and also promote their physical and spiritual health. Versed in green medicine, santeros and santeras regularly use plants in their work. These are often purchased from sites of urban agriculture. Each *orisha* is defined by specific characteristics, patronages, and plants. Some of the visible manifestations of this religion within the streets of Havana are people dressed in white with multi-coloured beads, *yerberías* (herb and religious paraphernalia markets), ceiba trees adorned with offerings, and brooms hung on doors (some of these symbols are shown in Figure 1.8). The rhythms of Santería rely on offerings for everyday maintenance and are inextricably linked to these gardens where the plants are often acquired.[53]

1.7 Research and Scholarship

Much of the research to date on urban agriculture in Cuba has focused on the history and specific organisation of the system. Ethnographic research surrounding sites of urban agriculture has focused on the power hierarchies associated with these spaces and the morality of food production. Isabelle Anguelovski's book *Neighborhood as Refuge: Community Reconstruction, Place Remaking, and Environmental Justice in the City* studies how social activism has been revealed through sites of urban agriculture and has precipitated positive change for communities. However, little attention has been paid to understanding how spaces of urban agriculture influence everyday

Figure 1.8 Symbols of Santería: wearing white and the ceiba tree where offerings are left

contemporary urban life in Havana. What is clear is that these ordinary spaces are neither explicitly public nor private but rather provide places for interactions to occur between diverse individuals. These connections take place within a space where things are cultivated, made, mixed, discussed, and sold, while the boundaries adjacent to these sites are shared and transgressed. Across these adjacencies, work, knowledge, goods, and conviviality are exchanged and combined, and these spaces emerge from quotidian practices and strategies. In his book *Geographies of Rhythm: Nature, Place, Mobilities and Bodies*, Tim Edensor outlined classes of rhythms that capture such practices.[54] Similarly, Filipa Wunderlich and others present several clear categories of urban rhythms in 'Symphonies of Urban Places: Urban Rhythms as Traces of Time in Space. A Study of "Urban Rhythms"'. These rhythms of urban space include social, cultural, natural, and sensorial rhythms.[55] Along with the outlined beats that are specific to Cuba, these rhythms facilitate the study of the diversity of Havana by revealing the temporal over the static and the experience of the city over its formal aspects.[56] While it is unclear how urban agriculture fits into the future development of the city, it undoubtedly identifies with urbanism, infrastructure, and landscape and falls somewhere in-between all three. Perhaps this position enables it to perform multiple roles within the city. James Corner, in 'Terra Fluxus', analysed the term landscape. Rather than solely providing respite in nature, he saw landscapes as contributing useful networks within the city and acting as a type of infrastructure to improve the wellbeing of the place.[57] This position of in-between also allows such sites to serve as urban instigators within the city—places where ideas get tried and tested and new ways of thinking about the metropolis are developed. Similar to how James Holston sees the self-building or 'autoconstruction' in the favelas of São Paulo, these sites of gardening create spaces for 'alternative futures', the everyday rhythms within these sites of urban agriculture become both the 'context and the substance' of the evolving city.[58] As infrastructures and instigators, such spaces make ever more vivid the polyrhythmic character of the city as they bring together the natural, cultural, economic, and social in an ecology that includes people and their everyday activities interacting together within communities throughout Havana.

1.8 Book Structure

The central concern of this book is to study and document the lived experiences surrounding sites of urban agriculture to construct a deeper understanding about the everyday life of Havana. To undertake this study, I have considered the quotidian rhythms and programmes of these sites and their surrounding communities (see Figure 1.10). To build capacity for this undertaking, I initially studied the body of literature surrounding everyday urban rhythms—rhythmanalysis—so as to identify a clear working method for the fieldwork and site assessment. I found that cities and their systems and networks are typically designed abstractly and at a distance and often pay little attention to people's ordinary lives. The existence of everyday and inter-related rhythms is rarely understood or considered. Chapter 2 uncovers the rhythmanalysis method used for analysing and documenting the sites through mapping. It reviews drift, layering, game-board, and rhizome as different tactics to study the sites of urban agriculture to identify and document their rhythms. Chapter 3 discusses the different perspectives and literature surrounding urban agriculture in Havana and the methods other researchers have used to study the contribution of these garden sites within the city. It identifies gaps in the existing research and suggests that the involvement of the everyday has not been used as a mechanism to develop a deeper understanding about the city of Havana.

Chapters 4 to 6 describe and document the everyday rhythms surrounding sites of urban agriculture in three different locations (Figure 1.5).

Together the written account and drawings uncover rhythms that depict the *oeuvre* of the place and the layered complexities of the everyday. Firstly, in Chapter 4, looking at San Isidro, the work reveals that the place is shaped by networks of cooperation and conviviality within the social, economic, and natural environment. These translate to the sharing of time and resources. Chapter 5 uncovers a site of urban agriculture in Cayo Hueso, Centro Habana, one of only three green spaces visible in the community. The site specialises in both plants used for herbal remedies, as medications are scarce, and also for spiritual use as many residents practice Santería. This chapter discusses the rhythms of everyday life within the surrounding neighbourhood, an area that has both the highest density and rate of deterioration in Cuba. Chapter 6 studies the rhythms surrounding a site of urban agriculture in Plaza de la Revolución, which exists in-between multiple government buildings, mid-rise towers, and fallow land. Finally, Chapter 7 reflects on the process and the findings of the research and suggests that a modified framework should be considered, one where urban studies consider the social, ecological, and economic everyday rhythms of a place in order to understand the intricacies of urban life more fully.

Figure 1.9 Working and relaxing in the garden in Cayo Hueso

Figure 1.10 Variety of programmes surrounding the sites of urban agriculture

Notes

1. Phoebe Lickwar and Roxi Thoren, *Farmscape: The Design of Productive Landscapes* (New York: Routledge, 2020), 2.
2. Lebbeus Wood, "Walls of Change," https://lebbeuswoods.wordpress.com/2010/05/28/walls-of-change/ (accessed October 2015).
3. Łukasz Stanek, "Methodologies and Situations of Urban Research: Re-Reading Henri Lefebvre's 'the Production of Space'," *Zeithistorische Forschungen/Studies in Contemporary History* 4 (2007): 462.
4. George Dodd, *The Food of London: A Sketch of the Chief Varieties, Sources of Supply, Probable Quantities, Modes of Arrival, Processes of Manufacture, Suspected Adulteration, and Machinery of Distribution of the Food for a Community of Two Millions and a Half* (London: Longman, Brown, Green, and Longmans, 1856).
5. Ash Amin and Stephen Graham, "The Ordinary City," *Transactions of the Institute of British Geographers* 22, no. 4 (1997): 411–429.
6. Jennifer Robinson, *Ordinary Cities: Between Modernity and Development* (London: Routledge, 2006), 64.
7. Stephan Barthel and Christian Isendahl, "Urban Gardens, Agriculture, and Water Management: Sources of Resilience for Long-Term Food Security in Cities," *Ecological Economics* 86 (2013): 224–234.

8. Filipa Wunderlich, "Place-Temporality and Rhythmicity: A New Aesthetic and Methodological Foundation for Urban Design Theory and Practice," in *Explorations in Urban Design: An Urban Design Research Primer*, ed. Mathew Carmona (Farnham: Ashgate, 2014), 63–64.
9. Ben Highmore, *Cityscapes: Cultural Readings in the Material and Symbolic City* (Basingstoke: Palgrave Macmillan, 2005), 146.
10. Gülçin Erdi Lelandais, ed., *Understanding the City: Henri Lefebvre and Urban Studies* (Newcastle upon Tyne: Cambridge Scholars Publishing, 2014), xii.
11. Łukasz Stanek, *Urban Revolution Now: Henri Lefebvre in Social Research and Architecture*, eds. Christian Schmid and Ákos Moravánszky (Burlington: Ashgate Publishing, 2014), 231.
12. Stanek, *Urban Revolution Now: Henri Lefebvre in Social Research and Architecture*, 31.
13. Henri Lefebvre, *The Production of Space* [La production de l'Espace], trans. Donald Nicholson-Smith (Oxford: Blackwell, 1991b), 33.
14. John Chase, Margaret Crawford and John Kaliski, *Everyday Urbanism* (New York: Monacelli Press, 1999), 29.
15. Stanek, *Urban Revolution Now: Henri Lefebvre in Social Research and Architecture*, 31.
16. Łukasz Stanek, *Henri Lefebvre on Space: Architecture, Urban Research, and the Production of Theory* (Minneapolis: University of Minnesota Press, 2011), 193.
17. David Harvey, *Rebel Cities: From the Right to the City to the Urban Revolution* (London: Verso, 2012), 4.
18. Chase, Crawford and Kaliski, *Everyday Urbanism*, 25–26.
19. Patricio del Real and Anna Cristina Pertierra, "Inventar: Recent Struggles and Inventions in Housing in Two Cuban Cities," *Buildings & Landscapes: Journal of the Vernacular Architecture Forum* 15 (2008): 78.
20. Pierre Sean Brotherton, *Revolutionary Medicine: Health and the Body in Post-Soviet Cuba* (Durham: Duke University Press, 2012), 86.
21. Felipe Hernández, Peter Kellett and Lea Allen, *Rethinking the Informal City: Critical Perspectives from Latin America* (New York: Berghahn Books, 2010), xi. Foreword by Rahul Mehrotra.
22. Robin James Smith and Kevin Hetherington, "Urban Rhythms: Mobilities, Space and Interaction in the Contemporary City," *Sociological Review* 61 (2013): 6.
23. Highmore, *Cityscapes: Cultural Readings in the Material and Symbolic City*, 145–146.
24. Ash Amin and Nigel Thrift, *Cities: Reimagining the Urban* (Cambridge: Polity, 2002), 19.
25. Henri Lefebvre, *Rhythmanalysis: Space, Time and Everyday Life*, trans. Stuart Elden and Gerald Moore (London: Continuum, 2004), 27–28.
26. Lefebvre, *Rhythmanalysis: Space, Time and Everyday Life*, 36.
27. Kurt Meyer, "Rhythms, Streets, Cities," in *Space, Difference, Everyday Life: Reading Henri Lefebvre*, ed. Kanishka Goonewardena, trans. Bandulasena Goonewardena (New York: Routledge, 2008), 155–156.
28. Stanek, *Henri Lefebvre on Space: Architecture, Urban Research, and the Production of Theory*, 86.
29. Stanek, *Henri Lefebvre on Space: Architecture, Urban Research, and the Production of Theory*, 278 note 38.

30. Thomas F. McDonough, "Situationist Space," *October* 67 (1994): 65.
31. Richard Brook, *Urban Maps: Instruments of Narrative and Interpretation in the City*, ed. Nick Dunn (Farnham: Ashgate, 2011), 11–12.
32. Lefebvre, *Rhythmanalysis: Space, Time and Everyday Life*, 15.
33. Ernesto Oroza, "Technological Disobedience: Ernesto Oroza," https://assemblepapers.com.au/2017/04/28/technological-disobedience-ernesto-oroza/ (accessed December 2021).
34. del Real and Pertierra, "Inventar: Recent Struggles and Inventions in Housing in Two Cuban Cities," 89.
35. Anke Birkenmaier and Esther Katheryn Whitfield, *Havana beyond the Ruins: Cultural Mappings after 1989* (Durham: Duke University Press, 2011), 78.
36. Ben Corbett, *This Is Cuba: An Outlaw Culture Survives* (Cambridge: Westview Press, 2002), 55.
37. Jill Hamberg, "Cuba Opens to Private Housing But Preserves Housing Rights," *Race, Poverty & the Environment* 19, no. 1 (2012): 74.
38. United States International Trade Commission, *Overview of Cuban Imports of Goods and Services and Effects of U.S. Restrictions* (Washington, DC: United States International Trade Commission, 2016), 10–11.
39. Mimi Whitefield, "Study: Cubans Don't Make Much, But It's More Than State Salaries Indicate," *Miami Herald*, www.miamiherald.com/news/nation-world/world/americas/cuba/article89133407.html#storylink=cpy (accessed 27 December 2016).
40. Office of Global Analysis, FAS, USDA, *Cuba's Food & Agriculture Situation Report 2008*, 24.
41. Anna Cristina Pertierra, *Cuba: The Struggle for Consumption* (Coconut Creek: Caribbean Studies Press, 2011), 50.
42. United States International Trade Commission, *Overview of Cuban Imports of Goods and Services and Effects of U.S. Restrictions*, 32.
43. International Cooperative Alliance, "What Is a Cooperative?," www.ica.coop/en (accessed 5 January 2019).
44. Jane Jacobs, Samuel Zipp and Nathan Storring, *Vital Little Plans: The Short Works of Jane Jacobs* (New York: Random House, 2016).
45. Marina Gold, *People and State in Socialist Cuba: Ideas and Practices of Revolution* (New York: Palgrave Macmillan US, 2015), 3.
46. Par Kumaraswami, *Rethinking the Cuban Revolution Nationally and Regionally: Politics, Culture and Identity* (Chichester: Wiley-Blackwell, 2012), 38.
47. Kumaraswami, *Rethinking the Cuban Revolution Nationally and Regionally: Politics, Culture and Identity*, 1.
48. Kumaraswami, *Rethinking the Cuban Revolution Nationally and Regionally: Politics, Culture and Identity*, 58.
49. Gold, *People and State in Socialist Cuba: Ideas and Practices of Revolution*.
50. Lefebvre, *The Production of Space*, 54.
51. Gold, *People and State in Socialist Cuba: Ideas and Practices of Revolution*, 15.
52. Gary Marx, "Getting One's Way on an Isle of Want," *Chicago Tribune*, sec. Letter from Havana, November 15, 2004, http://articles.chicagotribune.com/2004-11-15/news/0411150150_1_cubans-connections-friend (accessed 28 April 2018).
53. Gold, *People and State in Socialist Cuba: Ideas and Practices of Revolution*, 58–65.
54. Tim Edensor, *Geographies of Rhythm Nature, Place, Mobilities and Bodies* (Farnham: Ashgate, 2010), 4.

55. Filipa Wunderlich et al., "Symphonies of Urban Places: Urban Rhythms as Traces of Time in Space: A Study of 'Urban Rhythms'," *Studies in Environmental Aesthetics and Semiotics* 6 (2008): 104–105.
56. Alison Sant, "Redefining the Basemap," *Intelligent Agent* 6, no. 2 (2002), Interactive City, www.intelligentagent.com/archive/Vol6_No2_interactive_city_sant.htm.
57. James Corner, "Terra Fluxus," in *The Landscape Urbanism Reader*, ed. Charles Waldheim (New York: Princeton Architectural Press, 2006), 24.
58. James Holston, *Insurgent Citizenship: Disjunctions of Democracy and Modernity in Brazil* (Princeton: Princeton University Press, 2008), 8–9.

2   Studying and Documenting Everyday Urban Life

2.1 Introduction

For many that choose to study the city of Havana, there is a pressing sense that it is either '[o]ut of time, on a time of its own', or 'stuck in time', and there is an urgent need to grasp it before it slips through our hands and vanishes.[1] While it is clear that the city cannot continue along its current trajectory, it is not immediately apparent *what* it is that may disappear, but there is a feeling that there may soon be a profound sense of loss. As the buildings collapse or even when the ocean washes into the city, such as occurred on 10 September 2017, with Hurricane Irma, 'it' prevails. So, the 'it' being referred to here is not the crumbling formal city but the rhythms of everyday life. Nowhere is this more salient than within Havana's communities. Rather than treating a site as typological and morphological, studying its rhythms uncovers its *oeuvre*. These cannot be grasped in a singular way but, rather, walking through a community evokes the senses through the sounds, spaces, and smells that interweave its atmosphere and history. Recording these sensations through text, film, or photography over time uncovers an initial reading of a place. But what are needed are spatial studies that dig deeper into the rhythms of the city to uncover a more nuanced understanding of the place as multidimensional, heterogeneous, and complex. Along with Lefebvre, several other authors have used rhythms as a method to record and describe everyday urban life—so-called rhythmanalysis. While the methods vary, all remain embedded in an understanding that the researcher should be both part of the urban experience for the study and then distant from it for the analysis. Using Lefebvre's enigmatic and ephemeral instructions, scholars have conducted studies of particular places by mapping specific activities, analysing layers of history through film and written records, and measuring the sensorial qualities of a city to heighten an understanding of the everyday lived experiences and rhythms.

DOI: 10.4324/9781003201410-2

2.2 Rhythmanalysis: Space, Time, and Everyday Life

Elements of Rhythmanalysis was originally published in 1992 by René Lourau, after Lefebvre's death. This book consisted of a series of chapters that covered a broad range of subjects involving cities, movement, bodily rhythms, media, music, and the management of time, all of which focused on the study of rhythms. The book was later released as *Rhythmanalysis: Space, Time and Everyday Life;* this addition included two earlier essays: 'The Rhythmanalysis Project' and 'Attempt at the Rhythmanalysis of Mediterranean Towns' co-authored with Catherine Régulier.[2]

Lefebvre was interested in how different groups measured distinct attributes of rhythms. For example, economists work with financial cycles, athletes with movement, musicians with melody, and historians with epochs.[3] Each of these measurements are people, place, and context dependent. Measuring each of these rhythms poses challenges for researchers, especially when diverse tempos converge with one another. In addition, rhythms are either cyclical and derived from natural or cosmic processes, or linear and mechanised and part of exchanges or social practices. As these rhythms combine, they evoke conflict and harmony. *Arrhythmia* is Lefebvre's term for disturbance among rhythms; *polyrhythmia* is the broad combination of multiple rhythms without conflict; while *eurhythmia* is the uniting of rhythms within healthy systems such as the body.[4] The rhythmanalyst listens to both the 'silence' and the 'noise', so it can be 're-present[ed as] the interpretation' of the rhythms. This re-presentation is one of the unexplored strengths of rhythmanalysis—as a tool for analysis or design that has been largely overlooked.[5]

The rhythmanalyst uses their own body as a listening device and as a reference so they are actively part of a study where their senses serve as a type of metronome. Lefebvre described the process of rhythmanalysis and stressed the need to 'situate oneself simultaneously inside and outside' a study location, with the suggestion that a balcony would serve the purpose.[6] He described the scene from his apartment window on the Rue Rambuteau in Paris, across from the Pompidou Centre and how, from his slightly detached vantage point, he could distinguish between the harmonious and conflicting rhythms that included cars stopping and starting at a traffic light, the silence of pedestrians concentrating while crossing busy intersections, and the smell of exhaust fumes. He noticed the diverse pedestrian groups that walked at different times of the day, such as school children, shoppers, café patrons, and tourists. He included in this study a discussion of the cyclical rhythms of the weather and the seasons and how nature modified the beat of the city. Lefebvre believed that the state and its institutions imposed invisible rhythms that permeated everyday life. While they are barely discernible, it is the role of the rhythmanalyst to uncover these silently enforced rhythms of power.[7]

One such imposed rhythm is 'dressage'. Lefebvre related this practice to the training of humans and animals to behave in particular ways. Prevalent in business environments, sports, education, families, the military, and religion, dressage is imposed by breaking people in through ongoing training. The methods utilise 'duration, harshness, punishments and rewards'.[8] Lefebvre believed that dressage was prevalent in all aspects of life such that the body is ultimately shaped by society, with even the gait and manner of people evolving over time.[9] Daily life in Havana, as anywhere else, is certainly shaped by 'dressage'—much of it imposed by the government through laws and the education, provisioning, and healthcare systems.

Henri Lefebvre and Catherine Régulier published 'The Rhythmanalytical Project' in 1985. This paper set out all the themes for their later book. It summarised the relationship between linear and cyclical time. Linear time defines all of the parcelled aspects of our lives, including work, sleep, meals, and social time.[10] Linear time is intersected by cosmic and biological rhythms—such as the seasons and breathing. Many rhythms exist in-between linear and cyclical time, such as hunger or sleep; while both occur regularly, they are highly dependent upon customs and cultures. The collective composition of these rhythms defines the complexity of everyday life.

2.3 Other Studies of Rhythms

In 'Being a Rhythm Analyst in the City of Varanasi', Reena Tiwari used the strategy of layering different maps of Varanasi to gather fragments of this Indian city.[11] Some of the illustrations involved documenting her personal lived experiences and others came from existing cartographic information. Layering these multiple rhythms on a map holds much promise as a method to increase our understanding of the manifold experiences of the city. Similarly, Yi Chen, in her book *Practising Rhythmanalysis: Theories and Methodologies* sieved through accounts of the different rhythms she uncovered through texts and film. Reading and viewing multiple descriptions of a particular street, Brickyard Lane in London, highlighted diverse patterns associated with the community over time and related them to changes in government.[12] In 'Walking in the Multicultural City: The Production of Suburban Street Life in Sydney', Rebecca Williamson used her experience of walking within the city as a way to more fully comprehend ethnic identity.[13] Filipa Wunderlich studied the sensorial and performative characteristics of cities and developed a method for mapping and classifying different activities in a particular space.[14] Tim Edensor, in his Introduction to *Geographies of Rhythm: Nature, Place, Mobilities and Bodies*, recognised different types of rhythms including non-human rhythms.[15] He recognised that these can radically change a city and involve myriad activities, such as garbage collection, wildlife, and weather events.[16]

Kevin Lynch explored indicators of time and place in his book *What Time is this Place?* including decay, changing foliage, and festivities, that helped define a more sensorial reading of a city than do dates and times marked on calendars or clocks.[17] Collectively these authors have uncovered different temporal readings of the city that help to reveal the essence of urban life in a place.

2.4 Method of Study

Lefebvre and others have suggested that a rhythm-analytical study should integrate multi-sensory observations at different times of the day, week, or year at a particular site. The researcher must conduct their study in two ways: at a distance, without influencing the setting and then through immersion, to understand both the macro rhythms of a place as well as the minutia of its everyday life. There are also lessons inherent in the organisation of Lefebvre's *Rhythmanalysis: Space, Time and Everyday Life*, a book that supports a non-linear iterative methodology to layer an understanding of a place. The chapters of Lefebvre's book do not unfold sequentially; rather they suggest a study method that moves from the abstract to the concrete and from the concrete to the abstract.

For this to be a useful study, the selected sites should be representative of the rhythms of the city so as to make larger conclusions about Havana. The selected sites also need to represent contextual diversity. Once a specific place has been identified for study, it is important to distinguish the different rhythms to record. These should include both the ordinary and the extraordinary rhythms of a place. The study times within the sites need to be distributed across seasons, days, and hours so as to evaluate whether these rhythms are particular to a specific temporal period. A starting point for recording rhythms might include observing the following:

1. The senses and atmospheres surrounding the study site: visual, auditory, olfactory, and haptic.
2. The physical context surrounding the site: terrain, vegetation, typology, morphology.
3. Linkages between other institutions, systems, and networks surrounding the site.
4. Rules surrounding the site, such as traffic patterns or opening times of businesses.
5. Extraordinary everyday rhythms that occur hourly, daily, weekly, or yearly, such as festivals or parties.
6. The changing rhythms of the street materiality over time: building collapse, garbage distribution, animals roaming, vehicles, hanging laundry, temporary street signs (graffiti, for-sale signs, road works, etc.).

7. Structural changes of the site: the emergence and demise of businesses over the study period.
8. The movements of people, including different activities and resting.
9. Domestic rhythms such as cleaning, cooking, or washing that are visible to pedestrians in the street.
10. An understanding of the movements of the community—for example where do people buy provisions, go to school, or receive medical care? This information contextualises the community within the city.
11. The interactions of neighbourhood groups with authority and government: police activity, officials fumigating against mosquitoes, the Committee for the Defence of the Revolution (CDR), and garden inspectors.
12. Differences between rhythms of repetition and those of actual change.

Many of these are hard to depict just through writing, while others do not lend themselves to illustration or mapping. By adopting both methods of documentation, this book provides both a textual account of each site and a graphic one. The goals of this research are simultaneously theoretical, conceptual, and epistemological. The intention is to develop a method to study the sites in Havana while concurrently developing a rigorous process that could be used to inform comparative urbanism and design. This method measures the rhythms of a place as they tell us about everyday life; it also works as a design method for considering the future city. By studying the rhythms of the present, it should be possible to use it to re-imagine the future.

While there has been much use of rhythmanalysis for textual studies of sites and situations, it has not been used to build an understanding of a place to use for design. Cities and their systems and networks are usually designed abstractly and at a distance. Research is typically done at a macro scale, without following the small evolutions of a place over time. The existence of complex everyday rhythms is rarely understood or considered. A rhythmic analysis over a period of six years enabled me to measure the quotidian life of Havana. As I got close to these sites and understood how they were made and re-made I came to understand that there are lessons within them for the evolving city and studies of the everyday could become sources for future potential. Rhythmanalysis became the tool with which to understand these sites. The following methods are the different tactics used to *listen* and *record* the rhythms.

2.5 Recording Public Life

This study method used drawings as a way of recording urban life. These are used as an analytical and explanatory tool. The multiple layers on a map help us understand progressively how we see, inhabit, and characterise a city. More detailed orthographic drawings locate specific activities in plan and section. Jan Gehl and Brigitte Svarre presented very clear methods for recording the quantities of people in public spaces, through means that included counting and estimating their ages and genders, mapping their activities and locations in space, tracking people's movements throughout a site on a plan, and looking for traces by finding the actual marks in the city that indicated where and how people are moving.[18] William Whyte, in *The Social Life of Small Urban Spaces*, studied how people used space, through time-lapse photography which he used to record the everyday life around buildings. This enabled him to recount narratives about city spaces through the study of changing rhythms.

2.6 Mapping Urban Space

Maps of urban spaces describe the existing conditions while also offering new interpretations. 'J. B. Harley [...] argued that maps are social constructions of the world: "[...] that re-describe the world—like any other document—in terms of relations of power and of cultural practices, preferences, and priorities."'[19] Mapping is an activity that unites observation and understanding that is rooted within a time and a place. James Corner wrote a very influential paper on mapping: 'The Agency of Mapping. Speculation, Critique and Invention'. One of the obstacles Corner identified was that we use maps as representations and not as tools. He believed that the act of mapping should be used to study and reveal, to help us reimagine the world. Used in this way, maps are powerful instruments and, in his essay, Corner distinguished four methods in which practices of mapping could tease out different notions of time and space.[20] Each one requires uncovering data about the place, including climatic, social, physical, and political information. The four thematic methods are drift, layering, game-board (also called gameboard), and rhizome. Each offers access to different temporal and spatial understandings about a place (See Figure 2.3).

2.6.1 Drift

The drift (or *dérive*) method is based on a drawing by Paul-Henry Chombart de Lauwe, which showed a year in the life of a student living in the 16th Arrondissement of Paris. The drawing depicted her very limited triangular movements between her university residence, school, and piano classes.[21] This drawing inspired Guy Debord to make a *dérive*, a method that involved cognitive mapping of an urban site by walking around it to understand the everyday life of the city, beyond the official and documented. Developed by Debord and the Situationists and epitomised by the drawing entitled

The Naked City, in 1957, this mapping method incorporates an understanding that a city has different ambiances or character changes. From a *dérive* point of view, 'cities have psychogeographical contours' that appear to discourage entry into or exit from certain zones.[22] This feeling is personal and is how we perceive certain parts of the city in comparison to other areas. This type of mapping does not homogenise the city but understands there are profound shifts within it.[23] These psychogeographical drawings create an alternative way of thinking about the city, especially as they operate outside of any traditional architecture or planning mandate. This way of mapping the city is about understanding the embodied experiences of the city and disrupts our typical ways of understanding urban space.

Walker Evans produced some of his most famous images of urban life in May 1933 in Havana. During a three-week stay, he produced a series of photographs for *The Crime of Cuba*, a book by the American journalist Carleton Beals, who focused on uncovering the USA's exploitation of the citizens of Cuba. The goal of this book was to expose the corruption of the Cuban dictator Gerardo Machado, and Evans' photographs were a powerful accompaniment to the book's message. The result has been regarded as 'psychogeographical' as his photographs depicted 'the lived spaces of Havana'.[24] Telling a curated narrative of the city through a series of still images, while walking through communities continues to hold much promise and I have made similar walks through the streets of Havana that surround these sites so as to capture the city's lived rhythms through photography and drawings. Similarly, in *The Image of the City*, published in 1960, Kevin Lynch used cognitive mapping; but here, the maps are codifications of other people's perceptions of the cities, rather than his own sensations, and are more politically and emotionally neutral in intent.[25]

These types of drift mappings are all participatory. Despite the differences between the methods, they all demonstrate a remarkable degree of objectivity in the use of the human body and sensations to measure the qualities of urban space, and this holds much promise as a method for mapping the communities surrounding the sites. Drawings (often with accompanying photographs) are used throughout this book to document the quotidian activities that take place in Havana.

2.6.2 Layering

Layering involves 'superimposing otherwise independent layers of information' to understand the variety of data available about a city.[26] Designers have long been using layering as a device, both in the use of multiple layers of translucent tracing paper to sketch over drawings and in most digital drawing programmes.[27] As separate layers are overlaid, diverse relationships become visible. Surrounding these gardens, the layering of the morphology and the typology of the setting gives us a reading of the formal city, while the human activities make evident the lived condition. More specific to drawing spatial and temporal elements is the idea of the palimpsest. A palimpsest is a type of manuscript where multiple marks are incorporated over time so that they remain visible as subsequent layers are added. Havana can be understood as a palimpsest through its diverse layers, both the physical and the lived, which together construct Cuba's collective history.[28] An understanding of Havana as a palimpsest is useful to this rhythm-analytical exploration as the multiple layers weave together to create the urban *oeuvre*. Everywhere there are traces of the past within this city. Many buildings had their uses reassigned at the start of the Revolution. However, in many cases, the old signs still hang above doorways, or the original uses are etched in the mosaic tiles of a lobby floor. The Hospital Clínico Quirúrgico Hermanos Ameijeiras, in Cayo Hueso, occupies a building that was designed to be the National Bank of Cuba and the Stock Exchange, uses that no longer had any relevance after the Revolution. The grand entry is now emblematic of a public and accessible healthcare system rather than being symbolic of the power and wealth of capitalism. Likewise, schools inhabit many of the mansions of former rich American expatriates such that children spill out of classes held in some of the most impressive buildings in the city. The Presidential Palace has become the Museum of the Revolution, with the bullet holes still evident in the plaster. In fact, the walls of the city show many layers of lived experiences, especially when they are exposed after an adjacent building collapses to reveal the rhythm of the structure; the modifications to the walls; the textures of the paint that peels away from the masonry; and the encroachment of neighbours with their extended dwelling spaces, ventilation openings, or water tanks.

2.6.3 Game-Board

Game-board involves understanding the synergies among the multiple groups that are present within a community. It is opportunistic, time, and space dependent, and one of the most powerful influences both within and surrounding these gardens. Game-board is similar to layering, but it differs in that it is an enabler that acts as a facilitator for the daily processes within a community. By studying these spaces as being composed of overlapping rhythms of activities, it becomes possible to uncover the symbioses that exist between the different actors that enable new possibilities to emerge.[29]

Raoul Bunschoten outlined a detailed method for studying a city through what he called a 'pocket world'. This involves placing a frame around part

Layer: Construction by historical period

Layer: Building heights

Layer: Level of decay

Layer: Level of heritage importance

Layer: Typology

Layer: Sites of potential collapse

* Data provided by the Office of the Historian

Figure 2.1 Layering information in San Isidro

of a city to create an observational device that can be used to focus an investigation of a small part of a place to uncover a more precise view of it.[30] This research investigated urban agriculture through a series of Havana's 'pocket worlds' where the bracketed areas allowed for a study of the everyday spatial interactions and the associated networks of collaboration.[31] The urban rhythms evident within these bracketed areas linked different elements that demonstrated many symbiotic relationships between different people, processes, and products. Within and surrounding these sites, there is a game-board in operation which connects economic and social relationships to the larger networks of the city. These daily activities leverage possibilities and turn these cultivation spaces into hubs for exchange, composting, water collection, recycling, education, healthcare, and community engagement.

2.6.4 *Rhizome*

Gilles Deleuze and Félix Guattari, in their book *A Thousand Plateaus*, depicted the characteristics of rhizomes as 'open-ended and indeterminate'.[32] As a plant, the rhizome is fundamentally different from the hierarchical arrangement of a tree.[33] Similarly to a game-board, a rhizome map describes complex ecosystems. It does not depict a single attribute but portrays a combination of characteristics that include the formal and especially the informal city. A rhizome seeks to reimagine the possibilities that can come from breakages, disruptions, or items that start and stop, so as to make new connections.[34] This is particularly relevant to this research as these investigated sites in Havana have experienced and continue to experience changes due to everyday events that have profoundly affected these garden spaces and the city but that are often miniscule in scale and would not resonate on a conventional map. Almost impossible to depict, these include such events as garbage removal, its quantity, and the evolving damage to the city; or a site of collapse being overtaken by vegetation. In isolation, it is almost imperceptible, but when one adds these tiny events together and studies them over a period of several years, powerful trends start to emerge (for example, see Figure 4.11).

2.7 Mapping Method

The order of operations for this study involved recognising a 'pocket world' of activities (Figure 2.2) as this enabled a focused and precise view of the complex reality surrounding an urban agriculture site in Havana. The process involved making drawings of the context and marking on maps the exact uses of the buildings surrounding the sites. This was much harder than one might think. With no advertising and few commodities, furnishings, or

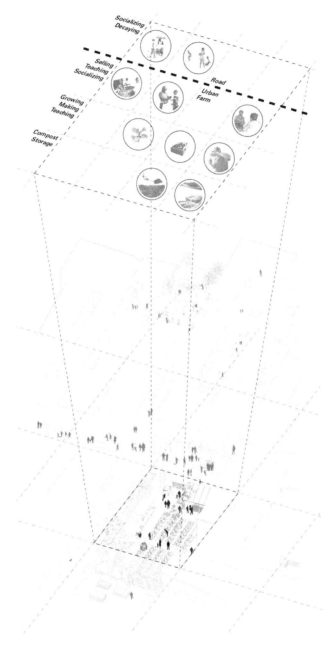

Figure 2.2 The extent of the pocket world and game-board of activities evident within San Isidro

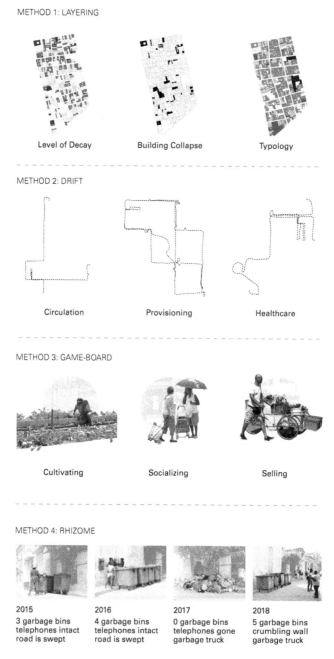

Figure 2.3 Flow diagram of the methodology

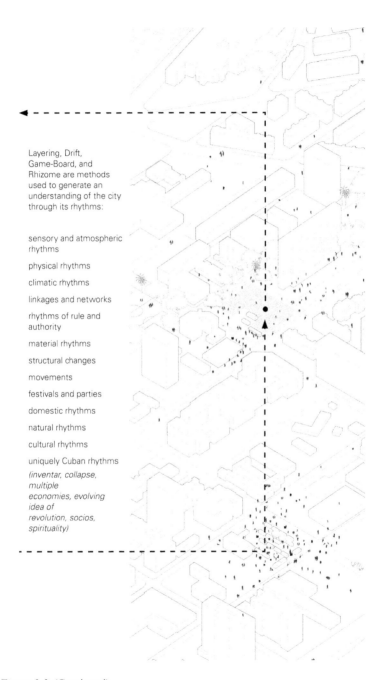

Layering, Drift,
Game-Board, and
Rhizome are methods
used to generate an
understanding of the city
through its rhythms:

sensory and atmospheric
rhythms

physical rhythms

climatic rhythms

linkages and networks

rhythms of rule and
authority

material rhythms

structural changes

movements

festivals and parties

domestic rhythms

natural rhythms

cultural rhythms

uniquely Cuban rhythms
*(inventar, collapse,
multiple
economies, evolving
idea of
revolution, socios,
spirituality)*

Figure 2.3 (Continued)

equipment, it was very difficult to recognise the precise nature of a business. The uses of buildings and spaces are often quite different from what one initially imagined. Informal interviews assisted with the process as they often revealed previously unimagined connections between people and places. Drawings, films, and photographs, together and separately, highlighted what was salient about a site. Precise as-built drawings of the surrounding buildings brought into view the evolving characteristics of living, working, playing, and growing. Sectional studies highlighted moments that were not previously understood in the plan. Making multiple loops of the site, from different directions, brought diverse realities into focus and highlighted the extent of the near and far networks of the game-board surrounding the site. Stopping and recording the site from both within the garden and at a distance uncovered different aspects. When this process was conducted at various times of the day, week, and year, it highlighted the qualities of the space across different seasons.

Observations at different times of day and year both within the garden and in the community uncovered different narratives about the sites. Sometimes these were hard to draw but were easier to describe through text. Others were easier to record through drawing. The specific mapping tactics previously described brought into focus different aspects about the place. Drift highlighted patterns of movement, limits, extents, and psychogeographical readings of a place; layering uncovered patterns of the place—especially over time and historical events; game-board revealed symbiotic relationships that existed within the community; and rhizome exposed associations between seemingly unrelated things. The text and mapping methods collectively revealed rhythms, not scientific ones but quotidian beats of everyday life, including sensory and atmospheric rhythms, physical (repetition of elements) and climatic rhythms, linkages and networks, rhythms of rule and authority, material rhythms, structural changes, movements, festivals and parties, and domestic, natural, cultural, and uniquely Cuban rhythms (inventar, collapse, multiple economies, evolving ideas about the Revolution, *socios*, and spirituality). Objects and functions have tended to be instrumental for describing the city. Maps that just depict these two attributes fail to capture the complexity of a city that operates between the formal and informal and its quotidian culture. This nascent multifaceted urban method recalibrates this way of thinking and demonstrates the importance of the sensorial and the everyday to comprehending the life of the city.

> [The] agency [of mapping] lies in neither reproduction nor imposition but rather in uncovering realities previously unseen or unimagined, even across seemingly exhausted grounds.[35]

Notes

1. Jose Quiroga, *Cuban Palimpsests* (Minneapolis: University of Minnesota Press, 2005), viii.
2. Meyer, "Rhythms, Streets, Cities," 147.
3. Meyer, "Rhythms, Streets, Cities," 148.
4. Lefebvre, *Rhythmanalysis: Space, Time and Everyday Life*, 16, 67.
5. Lefebvre, *Rhythmanalysis: Space, Time and Everyday Life*, 18.
6. Lefebvre, *Rhythmanalysis: Space, Time and Everyday Life*, 27.
7. Lefebvre, *Rhythmanalysis: Space, Time and Everyday Life*, 36.
8. Lefebvre, *Rhythmanalysis: Space, Time and Everyday Life*, 40.
9. Lefebvre, *Rhythmanalysis: Space, Time and Everyday Life*, 40.
10. Lefebvre, *Rhythmanalysis: Space, Time and Everyday Life*, 73.
11. Reena Tiwari, "Being a Rhythm Analyst in the City of Varanasi," *Urban Forum* 19, no. 3 (2008): 293.
12. Yi Chen, *Practising Rhythmanalysis: Theories and Methodologies* (London: Rowman & Littlefield International, 2017), 3.
13. Rebecca Williamson, "Walking in the Multicultural City: The Production of Suburban Street Life in Sydney," in *Walking in Cities: Quotidian Mobility as Urban Theory, Method, and Practice*, eds. Evrick Brown and Timothy Shortell (Philadelphia: Temple University Press, 2016), 23.
14. Wunderlich, "Place-Temporality and Rhythmicity: A New Aesthetic and Methodological Foundation for Urban Design Theory and Practice," 63.
15. Edensor, *Geographies of Rhythm Nature, Place, Mobilities and Bodies*, 4. Text in book quoted from Amin and Thrift.
16. Edensor, *Geographies of Rhythm Nature, Place, Mobilities and Bodies*, 9.
17. Kevin Lynch, *What Time Is This Place?* (Cambridge: MIT Press, 1972), 65.
18. Jan Gehl, *How to Study Public Life*, ed. Birgitte Svarre (Washington, DC: Island Press, 2013), 24.
19. Janet Abrams and Peter Hall, *Else/Where: Mapping New Cartographies of Networks and Territories* (Minneapolis: University of Minnesota Design Institute, 2006), 12.
20. James Corner, *The Landscape Imagination: Collected Essays of James Corner, 1990–2010*, ed. Alison Bick Hirsch (New York: Princeton Architectural Press, 2014), 197.
21. Guy Debord, "Theory of the Dérive," *Bureau of Public Secrets*, www.bopsecrets.org/SI/2.derive.htm (accessed May 2016).
22. Debord, "Theory of the Dérive."
23. McDonough, "Situationist Space," 65.
24. James Clifford Kent, "Walker Evans's Psychogeographic Mapping of Havana, 1933," *History of Photography* 37, no. 3 (2013): 326.
25. Michel de Certeau, *The Practice of Everyday Life* [L'Invention du Quotidien], trans. Steven Rendall (Minneapolis: University of Minnesota Press, 1998), 91–110.
26. Corner, *The Landscape Imagination: Collected Essays of James Corner, 1990–2010*, 223–224.
27. Corner, *The Landscape Imagination: Collected Essays of James Corner, 1990–2010*, 219.
28. Lynch, *What Time Is This Place?*, 171.
29. Lefebvre, *Rhythmanalysis: Space, Time and Everyday Life*, viii.

30. Raoul Bunschoten and Chora, *Urban Flotsam: Stirring the City* (Rotterdam: 010 Publishers, 2001), 111.
31. Bunschoten and Chora, *Urban Flotsam: Stirring the City*, 143.
32. Corner, *The Landscape Imagination: Collected Essays of James Corner, 1990–2010*, 227.
33. Gilles Deleuze and Félix Guattari, *A Thousand Plateaus: Capitalism and Schizophrenia*, trans. Brian Massumi (London: Continuum, 2004), 23.
34. Deleuze and Guattari, *A Thousand Plateaus: Capitalism and Schizophrenia*, 7–14.
35. Corner, *The Landscape Imagination: Collected Essays of James Corner, 1990–2010*, 197.

3   Different Perspectives Surrounding Urban Agriculture

3.1 Introduction

The collapse of the Soviet Union represented a profound shift in the rhythms of Cuban life. As Kevin Lynch discussed in *What Time is this Place?* such moments can devastate a city.[1] However, out of the crisis, urban agriculture emerged to facilitate the supply of food and green medicine. To date, much of the research on urban agriculture in Cuba has focused on the history of its implementation and evaluations of this system. This has included information about the organisation, the technological innovations associated with the system, and assessments of its successes and failures. Architects and planners have studied the constructed forms of specific sites of urban agriculture within Cuba. Some studies have also been done by sociologists, anthropologists, and urban geographers as to how these urban gardens are important neighbourhood socio-spatial and ecological infrastructures that contribute to the resilience of cities.[2]

These places have been investigated in several overlapping ways:

1. As a study of the different typologies of urban agricultural sites within the city
2. As a means of understanding environmental and spatial justice within communities advocating for access to fresh food and green medicine to improve the liveability of their neighbourhoods
3. As part of the everyday effort to provision in Cuba, along with the economics and moralities associated with that endeavour
4. As part of the hierarchies and struggles surrounding power that exists between producers, consumers, neighbours, and the state
5. As a part of a land-management system or planning policy within the city
6. As an expression of the evolving definition of the 1959 Revolution
7. As an expression of different cultural identities including Afro-Cuban religions

DOI: 10.4324/9781003201410-3

In aggregate, this list provides an initial understanding of the role sites of urban agriculture play as part of a national network of local food production within different contexts of urbanisation. The spatial studies of these sites have been dominated by formal analyses of the discrete gardens and none of the different lenses have comprehensively uncovered the polyrhythmic nature of everyday life within and surrounding these sites within the city.

3.2 Typologies of Urban Agriculture in Havana

Architects, planners, and urban designers are always interested in blurring the boundaries between the urban and the agrarian.[3] In fact, designers, including William Morris, Le Corbusier, Frank Lloyd Wright, and Ebenezer Howard, all have had their own version of an ideal city in which food production helped shape the urban realm.[4] Similarly, André Viljoen, Katrin Bohn, and Joe Howe's *Continuous Productive Urban Landscapes: Designing Urban Agriculture for Sustainable Cities* presented a vision for uninterrupted landscapes that integrated agriculture, recreation, and active transportation networks throughout the city. Through a series of essays, they discussed the ideas and issues surrounding this utopian implementation. These researchers chose Cuba as a laboratory in which to garner information and reveal potentialities for future European cities.

André Viljoen and Joe Howe documented ten sites within Havana, Cienfuegos, and Rodas, and outlined urban agriculture typologies at three different scales: the city, the town, and the village. Their idea was to try to catalogue the attributes of these spaces through drawings of the plans of the sites, and brief descriptions of the types of crops cultivated and the construction materials used to fabricate the growing beds. They did this through the use of single line section drawings and photographs and these all augmented our understanding of the constructed aspects of these sites. Jorge Peña Díaz and Phil Harris highlighted the different scales of these farms, from small back-yard gardens to larger neighbourhood sites, along with the associated social benefits. These qualities included the local access to fresh food, the transformation of derelict sites, and the introduction of vegetated spaces into the city.[5] In *Farming Cuba: Urban Agriculture from the Ground Up*, Carey Clouse expanded on this typological study through a cataloguing exercise.[6] She documented the characteristics of different sites, using a series of axonometric drawings. Throughout this book, the gardens' attributes are largely depicted as being separated from their surrounding urban contexts. While Clouse's study clearly demonstrated the different scales of farms, it did not uncover the context in which these sites existed, the networks with which they engaged, or the socio-spatial dynamics at the edge of these spaces where agriculture meets the city.

It is important to study the edge condition surrounding urban agriculture. This is the moment where the garden meets the people; this is the intersection where different co-located spaces and activities build on the agricultural activity.[7] The edge of these sites is also a place for observing and measuring the myriad, and often contradictory, everyday urban rhythms and sociospatial processes of the city. It is here, at the edge, where customers interact with the workers and cross the threshold to enter the garden. This is the zone where adjacent activities encroach or respect the property lines, where water is collected from adjacent roofs and piped into cisterns on the property, school children and the elderly access the site to learn, while governmental inspectors enter to scrutinise. It is here where the production of space surrounding these sites can be analysed by studying both the performative and experiential qualities of these places so as to understand the evolving rhythms that are made and re-made within these sites and their surrounding neighbourhoods.[8]

3.3 Environmental and Spatial Justice

In 'Cultivating Food as a Right to the City', Mark Purcell and Shannon K. Tyman argued that urban agriculture is an expression of spatial justice in the city.[9] Likewise, Isabelle Anguelovski's *Neighborhood as Refuge Community Reconstruction, Place Remaking, and Environmental Justice in the City* studied three neighbourhoods that have fought for community revitalisation, including Cayo Hueso, Havana; Casc Antic, Barcelona; and Dudley, Boston. Anguelovski studied the spaces citizens had created for recreation and health in their efforts to improve the liveability in each of these communities. These neighbourhoods had historically suffered environmental injustices within their localities and have had to cope with disproportionate amounts of dangerous and polluting infrastructures, along with minimal access to public spaces such as parks and playgrounds. These authors documented how the addition of urban farms and markets to these communities contributed both food and solidarity.[10] However, neither of these works unravelled the specificity of the urban environments or the quotidian practices and networks surrounding these places to present a fuller picture of such spaces within the city.

3.4 Everyday Economies and Moralities

The specificity of everyday life in Cuba is important and significant to this study. The country operates between multiple economies in a way that is very different from most other global communities. In addition, life in Cuba is always underscored 'by a variant of nationalism in which values such as self-sacrifice, hard-work and asceticism connect moralities of production to moralities of consumption'.[11] The state attempts to supply necessities to the Cuban population through a rationing system as it considers food to be an entitlement. However, the amount is woefully inadequate and people must supplement the state supply. So, food can be seen to be part of a system that involves individuals, communities, power, and resources that need to be explored both from the top down and the bottom up. Urban agriculture is part of this network and its moralities. Marisa Wilson, in *Everyday Moral Economies: Food, Politics and Scale in Cuba*, described how small-scale farmers (*parceleros*) in Cuba are richer than most state workers, unlike in most countries in the world, including other socialist societies, such as Vietnam and China. In addition, the *parceleros* have access to CUCs through selling high quality produce to the tourist industry. So, while small-scale farmers are not officially required to donate produce to the *acopio* (the 'state institution that re-distributes produce from farms for "social consumption"'[12]) but rather just grow local food, many do decide to donate. Wilson believes that this contribution is often part of this underlying morality or, at a more basic level, is intended to off-set community speculation that these farmers may be selfish or estranged from social interests, especially since the land they are working is often given in usufruct and belongs to the state.[13]

Michel de Certeau, in *The Practice of Everyday Life*, studied the spatial practices of ordinary people and how they negotiated the official city, manoeuvred through its rules and subverted them to make room in it for themselves.[14] Certeau used the analogy of the 'map' and the 'tour' where the map is described as a 'formal ensemble of abstract places', while the tour is associated with ordinary people being able to 'insinuate their countless differences into the dominant text'[15] and engage privately within the map.[16] This is comparable to citizens negotiating a 'series of circulating networks'[17] for provisioning their everyday food and pharmaceuticals within multiple economies (Figure 1.7). These networks have a spatiality that is important to study to more fully understand the social production of these sites within the community. The multiple complex rhythms of these sites are embedded within the processes and practices of the city.

3.5 Political and Power Hierarchies

For citizens in Cuba, equal access to education, healthcare, housing, and food were the key platforms of a Revolution that successfully managed to eliminate illiteracy, homelessness, many tropical diseases, and malnutrition.[18] However, ordinary Cubans experienced evolving state policies, not just as political ideas but through daily practices such as buying food for meals or trying to get medicine to treat an ailment, meaning that 'power is produced and reproduced in the interstices of daily life'.[19]

Asif Hossain: Mixing medicine in garden, 2015

Carrying food to sell in the street

Activities in the street

Figure 3.1 Everyday life surrounding the site in San Isidro

Graphics by Stavros Kondeas, Rita Wang, Alicia McDowell (Gilmore), and Lucas McDowell

Adriana Premat supported this hypothesis.[20] In *Sowing Change: The Making of Havana's Urban Agriculture*, she challenged the predominant top-down perspectives from which urban agriculture has often been analysed with the state depicted as the enabler; instead, she studied the grass roots and bottom-up dynamics within Havana's urban agriculture.[21,22] Premat backed her analysis with a discussion of Lefebvre's spatial triad within the production of these spaces. Lefebvre's triad offers interesting insights, as he 'does [not] presume fixed relationships among them'.[23] Indeed, this framework sheds light on the evolving power struggles and multiple actors within these sites of urban agriculture, including government officials, neighbourhoods, producers, and customers within Havana. In her research, she offered a dialectic understanding of the opposing ideologies and values— privilege and access to provisions versus the revolutionary ideals of collective property, hard work and self-sacrifice.[24] Just as the Victory Gardens of World War II in the UK, Canada, and the USA mobilised individuals to self-provision and these efforts were seen to further the war effort, so Cubans have been encouraged to grow vegetables to counteract the hardships of the Special Period not just for their families but also for Cuba.[25] Whether the Cuban communities feel this has been adequately accomplished on land within their neighbourhoods had an impact on whether the usufruct land tenure system and the social relationships around it were allowed to continue. These sites must be seen to continually contribute to their neighbourhoods, or they risk being reclaimed by the state for alternative uses, such as housing or tourism. Far from being just sites of food production, these landscapes must continually ingratiate themselves within their communities. This exposes political, spatial, and social complexities that do not focus solely on access to food and the ability to cultivate but also on fulfilling a more pressing need within their neighbourhoods.[26]

Sinan Koont, in *Sustainable Urban Agriculture in Cuba*, outlined how all urban agricultural activities are assessed and evaluated by the Grupo Nacional de Agricultura Urbana, with quarterly site inspections of facilities.[27] Multiple government agencies are involved in these sites. They have devised evaluation criteria based upon 28 assessment categories, which involve the diversity of crops, best practices for animal husbandry, and support strategies, all of which Koont outlined in detail. Such inspections often force producers to modify their activities so as to meet the stipulated outcomes. However, neither Premat nor Koont's research identified the spatial changes made to accommodate these directives, the adaptive reuse (*inventar*) of materials in the garden, or the forged networks within the neighbours and communities. While Premat uncovered the nuanced changing landscapes of power through conversations and observation, her work did not focus on the evolving spatial changes that affected the communities surrounding these sites of urban agriculture. While the ethnographic research, in this study, captured the spirit of particular events within the community through text, it did not spatially record the many rhythms that contributed to the complexity of urban life surrounding these sites.

3.6 Land Management

The introduction of vegetation to create shade and cooler microclimates in the dense city has been an ongoing concern for the city of Havana. The French landscape architect, Jean Claude Forestier, saw this as one of the most urgent issues for the city and he presented a series of masterplans to address the 'balance between nature and the built form'.[28] His plans have been partially implemented, and his unrealised proposals have continued to influence city planners and the city's relationship to nature. In 1966, the Havana Belt was established as a green zone, with fruit trees, coffee, and dairy farming. Citizens participated, on a voluntary basis, in cultivating seedlings and preparing the soil, in the city's first official rendition of urban agriculture. Kevin Lynch in *What Time is this Place?* explored the human sense of time, a rhythm that is often different from the official or regulated time. Lynch believed that cultivating this land in Havana was 'ideological: to bring city people in contact with the country and with rural labour, to give them a sense of communal achievement, to integrate work and leisure'. He believed that it enabled the countryside to extend back into the city.[29] Since then, the development of urban agriculture has continued to spread, with local governments facilitating access to land for cultivation and subsidies for the purchase of seeds. The Ministry of Agriculture provides technical support and local farmers groups share practical experiences.[30] The aim is to have these sites motivated by altruistic activities and moral incentives, rather than purely for financial gain, as this activity is intended to be embedded within the public good.[31]

Several authors have discussed land management and ownership as being instrumental to supporting citizens' access to agricultural land. The Physical Planning Directorate and the Grupo Para el Desarrollo Integral de la Capital (Group for the Integral Development of Havana) are involved in the development of urban agriculture in the city. The former addresses capacity and zoning issues and the latter is involved with organising community groups through Talleres de Transformación Integral de Barrio (Workshops for the Integral Transformation of the Neighbourhood) to facilitate the creation of neighbourhood gardens.[32] Since 1994, the Ministry of Agriculture (MINAG) has had an urban agriculture department. The ministry works with the Provincial Offices of the People's Council and provides support services and material resources. Most importantly, it organises access to land. Citizens are encouraged to request unused land for cultivation. If the land is privately owned, then the delegates of the People's Council, who represent local agriculture, notify the legal owner of their intention to grant the land-use rights to the local gardener who plans to produce food on it. If the owner objects, then they have six months to start cultivating the land themselves. If they do not commence agricultural activities, then the rights are granted to the person who had requested them, but solely for the purpose of growing food.[33] Only structures necessary for cultivation can be built on the land. In addition, in 1997, with the adoption of Resolution No. 527/97 'urban dwellers can receive up to one-third of an acre as a personal lot in the periphery of the major cities'.[34] This has been maintained through the land reforms of 2008 and the Lineamientos of 2011, with the Cuban government continuing to support local agriculture in order to increase national food production. While these land reforms have facilitated access to land for new and existing farmers, the availability of agricultural inputs (seeds, seedlings, and water) is becoming increasingly more expensive.[35]

This temporary transfer of land stewardship to prioritise food production is possible, in part, due to the precarious nature of land ownership. Most citizens do not have any title to their property and when a building collapses, any rights to the property are relinquished to the government.[36] At the outset of the Revolution, many middle- and upper-class Cubans fled, thereby leaving their homes vacant. After the Revolution, the Ministry of Recovery of Misappropriated Goods redistributed this property to poor families. Many buildings also assumed new social roles, with the buildings of the wealthy, the elite, and foreigners being re-purposed as schools, hospitals, and housing. After 1959, all public utilities and private industries were also nationalised. All of this made land ownership and its use more fluid.[37]

María Caridad Cruz and Roberto Sánchez Medina, in *Agriculture in the City a Key to Sustainability in Havana, Cuba*, documented the evolution and future possibilities of land for urban agriculture. They studied the long-term potential for including urban agriculture within Havana, focusing specifically within two areas: Parque Metropolitano de La Habana and Consejo Popular Camilo Cienfuegos. The former, located along the Almendares River, has been a site of agriculture since the eighteenth century and has very low housing density; the latter is situated across the bay in a suburb that was developed after the Revolution. It has a population of 11,000, living in apartment buildings surrounded by acres of land. Cruz and Medina's multi-disciplinary research team reviewed the crops, livestock, demographics of workers, various land-uses of the neighbourhood, marketing practices, water sources, and the use of organic matter, with the intention that their book would become part of a process for facilitating improvements in the evolving system. The evaluations of each of these areas involved interviews complemented by participant observations of people cultivating the land.[38] The conclusions situated urban agriculture as providing food sovereignty and security and enhancing local economies. There was consensus that gender issues and the contribution of these sites to informal economies required further exploration. The ongoing use of domestic water at the sites was also seen as unsustainable. Thorough and informative, the research did not address the everyday spatial practices or the networks surrounding these sites that were brought about by urban agricultural activities.

Alejandro Arrechea Jiménez is a planner involved with Dirección Provincial de Planificación Física Ciudad de La Habana (DPPFCH), an organisation that focuses on policies and regulations within the Havana Planning Office and the Master Plan for Havana including industry and agriculture. He talked with me and my students about the future strategy for urban farming in Havana. He described the city in terms of three concentric circles that surround the core: the Central Zone is the most densely populated portion of the city and includes the historical centre; a second Intermediate Zone consists of more suburban density; and a third, the Peripheral Zone, primarily comprises agricultural land (Figure 1.3). Arrechea acknowledged that the Special Period urged citizens to use vacant land for food production in all of these zones. The people were supported with subsidised seeds, basic tools, and identified irrigation sources. He admitted that this programme was more successful than anticipated and improved the liveability of the whole city by cleaning up abandoned sites and introducing fresh food close to where people lived. He stated that in the future the planning office may not support urban agriculture in the centre of the city due to the development of other more *urban assets* such as tourism and the pressing need for housing. Arrechea stressed that the culture and identity of the place also have to be considered. He felt that agriculture will not be part of the future, more urban character the government would like to see as Havana's image.[39]

3.7 The Evolving Revolution

In her book, *Revolution, People and State in Socialist Cuba: Ideas and Practices of Revolution*, Marina Gold explored the concept of the Revolution in Cuba as being ongoing, realised through everyday praxis, and involving urban agriculture, alternative medicine, and *cuentapropistas*. This is in sharp contrast to an analysis of these gardens not being part of the emerging character of Havana or to Premat's suggestion that small-scale gardens somehow subvert the Revolution. The altruistic activities of supplying pharmaceutical products and food to citizens, the enhanced ecological sustainability of the city, and producers donating time to teaching classes at schools might be considered some of the most profoundly revolutionary practices happening within the city. While these quotidian activities are independent of the state, they help alleviate everyday struggles. For Cubans, the Revolution supplied subsidised housing and food and free healthcare and education, but it failed to deliver fully on many of the everyday necessities. These new revolutionary undertakings—that fall outside conventional state-sanctioned practices—help address these requirements through everyday networks and relationships.

3.8 Cultural Identity

Historically, Alexander von Humboldt's physical and cultural study of Cuba, in his book *The Island of Cuba*, was instrumental to understanding the botany, geography, commerce, and geology of the island.[40] Sugar and tobacco have profoundly shaped Cuba's landscape and history as much as any other criteria. Fernando Ortiz's *Cuban Counterpoint: Tobacco and Sugar*, published in 1940, presented two narratives of Cuban history: one expressed the counterpoint between tobacco and sugar; the other was a historical enquiry showing the importance of these two crops in developing the Cuban economy. Depicting tobacco and sugar as both agricultural products and social characters allowed Ortiz to examine the converging cultures that were brought together through colonialism in a process for which he developed the term 'transculturation'.[41] This term is still used to describe a culture's connection to a place (through plants). These sites of urban agriculture often specialise in the religious and medicinal plants the locals request, and the specificity of this vegetation actually uncovers much about the preferences and demographics of the people. In *Cuban Intersections of Literary and Urban Spaces*, Marina Gold noted that 'the largest bulk of clients in herbal gardens are *Santería* practitioners'. In addition, the producers are encouraged to have some training in herbal medicine, which is currently a viable alternative to Cuba's medical system. Due to the shortages of medications in the pharmacies, doctors refer their patients to knowledgeable urban farmers who sell herbs, give advice, and provide products for their patients' ailments. The Special Period forced the Ministry of Public Health to incorporate natural medicine into their repertoire of services as a result of the crisis, making these sites part of the city's extended health system.[42]

3.9 Towards a Spatial Study of Urban Agriculture

From these studies, it can be understood that agriculture in the urban realm has been, and still is, a technical achievement in Cuba that has been helping to feed the population since the Special Period. This system brings food production, which has largely become a commodity in the Western world and absent from public life, back into the urban realm as a visceral experience. The conspicuous characteristics of these sites within the city combine spatial, social, economic, political, cultural, health, and environmental networks within the city.

The official system of urban agriculture has been well researched and documented, particularly in respect to training and education, research and development, and provisions and inputs. In many ways this information is not an urban concern. The evolving moralities and politics of theses spaces have also been examined. However, the entwining of the everyday societal and spatial relationships that create the lived experiences of the urban spaces surrounding these sites of agriculture have largely not been studied. This is where this book's contribution lies. This book studies the rhythms of these sites to support James Holston's claim that such small actions within cities have the potential to become the 'site[s] and the substance [...] of its emergent forms'.[43] As will be seen in the following chapters, these small sites of insurgence within the community are a neighbourhood infrastructure: centres of food and medicine production linked to the social, economic, and ecological everyday activities of the neighbourhoods that contribute to the resilience of the city.[44]

Notes

1. Lynch, *What Time Is This Place?*, 3.
2. Barthel and Isendahl, "Urban Gardens, Agriculture, and Water Management: Sources of Resilience for Long-Term Food Security in Cities," 224–234.
3. Charles Waldheim, "Notes towards a History of Agrarian Urbanism," in *Bracket 1: On Farming—Almanac 1*, eds. Mason White and Maya Przybylski (Barcelona: Actar, 2010), 18.
4. Carolyn Steel, *Hungry City: How Food Shapes Our Lives* (London: Chatto & Windus, 2008).
5. André Viljoen, Katrin Bohn and J. Howe, *Continuous Productive Urban Landscapes: Designing Urban Agriculture for Sustainable Cities* (Boston: Architectural Press, 2005).
6. Carey Clouse, *Farming Cuba: Urban Agriculture from the Ground Up* (New York: Princeton Architectural Press, 2014), 76.
7. Edward W. Soja, *Postmodern Geographies: The Reassertion of Space in Critical Social Theory* (London: Verso, 1989), 80.
8. Jane Jacobs, *The Death and Life of Great American Cities* (New York: Random House, 2002), 50.
9. Mark Purcell and Shannon K. Tyman, "Cultivating Food as a Right to the City," *Local Environment* (2014): 2.
10. Isabelle Anguelovski, *Neighborhood as Refuge Community Reconstruction, Place Remaking, and Environmental Justice in the City* (Cambridge: MIT Press, 2014), 8.
11. Marisa L. Wilson, *Everyday Moral Economies: Food, Politics and Scale in Cuba* (Chichester: Wiley Blackwell, 2014), 186.

12. Wilson, *Everyday Moral Economies: Food, Politics and Scale in Cuba*, 161.
13. Wilson, *Everyday Moral Economies: Food, Politics and Scale in Cuba*, 166.
14. Fran Tonkiss, *Space, the City and Social Theory: Social Relations and Urban Forms* (Cambridge: Polity, 2005), 114.
15. de Certeau, *The Practice of Everyday Life*, xxii.
16. Javier Corrales, "Cuba's 'Equity without Growth' Dilemma and the 2011 *Lineamientos*," *LAPS Latin American Politics and Society* 54, no. 3 (2012): 34.
17. Amin and Thrift, *Cities: Reimagining the Urban*, 92.
18. Lee Dawdy Shannon, "'La Comida Mambisa': Food, Farming, and Cuban Identity, 1839–1999," *New West Indian Guide* 76, nos. 1 & 2 (2002): 48.
19. Marina Gold, "Urban Gardens: Private Property or the Ultimate Socialist Experience?," in *Cuban Intersections of Literary and Urban Spaces*, ed. Carlo Riobó (Albany: State University of New York Press, 2011), 28.
20. Adriana Premat, "State Power, Private Plots and the Greening of Havana's Urban Agriculture Movement," *City & Society* 21, no. 1 (2009): 29.
21. Adriana Premat, *Sowing Change: The Making of Havana's Urban Agriculture* (Nashville: Vanderbilt University Press, 2012).
22. Premat, "State Power, Private Plots and the Greening of Havana's Urban Agriculture Movement," 30.
23. Premat, "State Power, Private Plots and the Greening of Havana's Urban Agriculture Movement," 30.
24. Wilson, *Everyday Moral Economies: Food, Politics and Scale in Cuba*, 4.
25. Charles French, "The Social Production of Community Garden Space: Case Studies of Boston, Massachusetts and Havana, Cuba" (Durham: PhD, University of New Hampshire, 2008), 68.
26. Gold, "Urban Gardens: Private Property or the Ultimate Socialist Experience?," 33.
27. Sinan Koont, *Sustainable Urban Agriculture in Cuba* (Gainesville: University Press of Florida, 2011), 41.
28. Joseph L. Scarpaci, Roberto Segre and Mario Coyula, *Havana: Two Faces of the Antillean Metropolis* (Chapel Hill: University of North Carolina Press, 2002), 67.
29. Lynch, *What Time Is This Place?*, 28.
30. María Caridad Cruz and Roberto Sánchez Medina, *Agriculture in the City a Key to Sustainability in Havana, Cuba* (Kingston: Ian Randle Publishers, 2003), 24.
31. Koont, *Sustainable Urban Agriculture in Cuba*, 108.
32. Cruz and Medina, *Agriculture in the City a Key to Sustainability in Havana, Cuba*, 160.
33. Miguel Altieri et al., "The Greening of the 'Barrios': Urban Agriculture for Food Security in Cuba," *Agriculture and Human Values* 16, no. 2 (1999): 134.
34. Fernando Funes, *Sustainable Agriculture and Resistance: Transforming Food Production in Cuba* (Oakland: Food First Books, 2002).
35. Friedrich Leitgeb, Sarah Schneider and Christian Vogl, "Increasing Food Sovereignty with Urban Agriculture in Cuba," *Agriculture and Human Values* 33, no. 2 (2016): 415.
36. Daniel Fisher, "Cuba Opening Could Reopen Fight over Billions in Seized Property," *Forbes*, sec. Finance, 2014, www.forbes.com/sites/danielfisher/2014/12/18/cuba-opening-could-mean-mother-of-all-property-disputes/#8fcdab636c76 (accessed April 2016).

37. Henry Louis Taylor, *Inside El Barrio: A Bottom-Up View of Neighborhood Life in Castro's Cuba* (Sterling: Kumarian Press, 2009).

38. Cruz and Medina, *Agriculture in the City a Key to Sustainability in Havana, Cuba*, 19.

39. Alejandro Arrechea Jiménez, "Dirección Provincial de Planificación Física Ciudad de La Habana" (talk presented to Dalhousie University Havana Studio, Havana, Cuba, October 5, 2015).

40. Alexander von Humboldt, *The Island of Cuba*, ed. John Sidney Thrasher (New York: Negro Universities Press, 1969).

41. Fernando Ortiz, *Cuban Counterpoint, Tobacco and Sugar* (Durham: Duke University Press, 1995).

42. Gold, "Urban Gardens: Private Property or the Ultimate Socialist Experience?," 34.

43. Holston, *Insurgent Citizenship: Disjunctions of Democracy and Modernity in Brazil*, 23.

44. Barthel and Isendahl, "Urban Gardens, Agriculture, and Water Management: Sources of Resilience for Long-Term Food Security in Cities," 224–234.

4 Symbiotic Urban Rhythms in San Isidro

4.1 Introduction

Shaped by many different eras, Cuba was inhabited by the Taínos, the Ciboneys, and the Guanajatabeyes people; it was subjugated, ruled, and developed by the Spanish; modernised, operated, and controlled by the United States; freed from dictatorship by the triumph of the Revolution in 1959; and influenced by ideologies and subsidies from the Soviet Union until the dissolution of the Bloc in the early 1990s. The Partido Comunista de Cuba (Communist Party of Cuba) currently governs the country and has been in continual power since 1965. The design of the capital city of Havana has been significantly influenced by each of these epochs. Currently the city is decaying due to scarcities that can be partially attributed to the United States' ongoing political and economic blockade. This was momentarily thawed by Barack Obama in 2016, only to be reintroduced by the Trump administration in 2017. In 2019, Cuba implemented the so-called *Coyuntural* (temporary) measures that marked the first major recession since the end of the Special Period. Covid-19 and the lack of tourists have been profoundly difficult for the country's economy. The change in 2008 from the rule of Fidel Castro to the leadership of his brother, Raúl, and now to Miguel Díaz-Canel have led to progressive changes in Cuba that have raised large questions about its political, economic, social, and cultural future. Shifts in the currency, property ownership, remittances, the freedom of travel, and business development suggest evolving shifts in the everyday urban rhythms of the city of Havana. Protests in 2021 have only added to this uncertainty and the next layer of Cuba's palimpsestic history is unclear.

Transformations in everyday rhythms have always created insecurity, along with social and spatial change in cities over time. Friedrich Engels experienced this in industrial Manchester as he documented the changing conditions among the this city's working class.[1] Similarly, the mass

DOI: 10.4324/9781003201410-4

production of goods led to the rapid expansion of metropolises in Asia, Latin America, and Africa and the rural-to-urban migrations that resulted from this radically changed these countries' urban landscapes.[2] Robert Park and Louis Wirth's observations on the 'shifting patterns of immigration and residency in Chicago'[3] led them to try to formulate an urban theory that they believed could be applicable to all cities, based upon size, density, and heterogeneity.[4] However, it is impossible to create a coherent reading of a city that is produced and re-produced through different everyday rhythms and histories that emerge and dissipate to continually transform its urban realm. But it is possible to understand the patterns of specific moments, through a series of focused case studies. While each case study will show multiple and different rhythms, the polyrhythmic nature of each study will produce knowledge of the broader urban experience or at least provide a snapshot of a particular city at a certain moment in time. Certainly, not strictly scientific, rhythmanalysis is 'a form of social and cultural phenomenology' that gives us an understanding of 'what is most pervasive, most alive and most critical in everyday life' within a community.[5]

Lefebvre was not entirely clear on how to pursue this type of study, although we know the rhythmanalyst has to be present and part of the rhythms within the street and then be removed from it to analyse it.[6,7,8] These different perspectives between participation and distance and practice and research make rhythmanalysis a clear methodology for studying a neighbourhood and using it to leverage an understanding of the lived experiences of a place, especially when the study is conducted over time. Such an approach is not nostalgic or sentimental but rather inclusive and evocative. Rather than concentrating on the formal, static, and visual, which often tell us little about an informal city such as Havana, rhythmanalysis leads to an understanding of the performative and haptic *oeuvre* of everyday urban life. This chapter focuses on the rhythms that surround a site of urban agriculture in San Isidro, in the municipality of La Habana Vieja. The garden provides local access to food and green medicine and plays a part in alleviating this community's daily struggle for provisions.

4.2 The Community

Walking along Habana Street, in San Isidro, in the intense heat and humidity is a visceral and kinetic experience. The visceral includes olfactory, somatic, auditory, and haptic sensations, while the kinetic manifests itself in a street life that is in constant motion. Against the milieu of scarcity, the slow decay of infrastructure and the sudden collapse of buildings, is the resourcefulness of everyday invention in a city that continually 'modifies and reinvents itself' through everyday life.[9] It is impossible to try to construct an intelligible, rational city from this informality, but it is easy to identify some of the urban patterns that encompass 'particularities and similarities, repetition and difference, rupture[s] and continuities'.[10] In fact, the act of walking actively entails encountering these patterns: manoeuvring between ever-changing inanimate and animate objects; negotiating the unevenness of the decayed surfaces and the narrowness of the sidewalks and streets, while avoiding the strewn garbage and stagnant puddles of water; dodging between people, fruit and vegetable carts, bicycle taxis, and dogs; ducking when water drips from air conditioners, laundry, and other nameless sources above; and glimpsing views of everyday life through the fragile doorway grilles that separate the street from the home. De Certeau linked meaningful space in the city to the practice of walking and it was through walking that I first encountered these gardens within the city.[11]

One such site is in the south of La Habana Vieja, a UNESCO World Heritage Site, but this garden is outside of any published tourist itinerary. La Habana Vieja, as a whole, has an area of four square kilometres.[12] San Isidro is to the south of La Habana Vieja and is bounded by Merced on the north, Calle Egido to the west, and Desamparados to the south and east. This community was ironically named after a protector of market gardens and cultivated fields and was where dock and railroad workers historically lived in *solares* (rooming houses).[13] These typologies still comprise much of the housing stock but now accommodate whole families within a single room. The narrow streets, in this dense eighteenth-century neighbourhood, form the public spaces of the community with '11,385 residents living in about 1,384 dwelling units'.[14] The morphology of La Habana Vieja consists of connected houses that have high ceilings and inner courtyards for ventilation. The buildings are situated along narrow streets that provide shade at certain times of the day. This was a Spanish design solution for hot and dry climates, but it is not so favourable for the sunny humid conditions found in Havana, especially since occupants have taken over many of the ventilation shafts and have in-filled the tall floors with mezzanines in a desperate struggle to gain extra space for dwelling.[15,16] In addition, the ratio of green space to the population in this part of the city is incredibly low. The vegetated spaces are so few that a heat-island effect occurs, where the district is nearly always warmer than the surrounding city.[17] The area was made a World Historic Heritage site in 1982 but restoration progressed slowly. In 1993, Havana's Office of the Historian was granted the right to access the district's affiliated profit-making companies, such as retail shops, museums, restaurants, bars, and hotels, and to use part of the money to reinvest in restoring the historic district.[18] This has been very successful for tourism in the area. However, from 1972 to 2002, the population steadily decreased from 176,030 to 96,763 inhabitants, with the displacement of the community having taken place almost entirely from within the renovated tourist sector in the north rather than from within San Isidro.[19] This trend continues as in 2020 the population was 80,738.[20]

4.3 The Garden

Within San Isidro there is a small garden that cultivates plants for food and medicinal and spiritual purposes. It occupies the space where a house collapsed circa 1990. During the Special Period of the 1990s, the land was used for food production within the community. However, one day in 2011, while the municipality was undertaking repair work in the street, the city inadvertently disconnected the site's domestic water supply. Immediately, the producers had to transition to crops that required less irrigation. The plants that are currently cultivated are used in Santería religious ceremonies—the rituals involve the use of herbs, roots, and flowers. These plants are also used in homeopathic remedies, or what is called green medicine, for their healing properties and include species such as moringa tree, basil, chija, oregano, garlic, cotton, ginger, hibiscus, and aloe vera. According to the gardeners, the site's shady, dry conditions support these plants. Customers now come from all over the city to this cultivated area to purchase its products and seek medical advice.

A lockable gate separates the site from the street (see Figure 4.1). The hours posted for consultations are between 10am and 2pm, from Monday to Friday, although this changes from time to time. Green medicine is endorsed by the medical community and is used in conjunction with conventional treatments. While there is ample access to doctors and pharmacies in Cuba, drugs are scarce and, to fill the void, physicians encourage their patients to use herbal remedies. The producer, Julio, gives customers medical advice on the plants he grows as he stands behind a mobile counter, which he wheels into place at the front of the garden during the hours of operation. He also sells products from other local farms at his point-of-sale counter; thus, connecting the site to the extended local economy. His part-time assistants help collect leaves, flowers, and roots from the various plants, while Julio carefully mixes or wraps the medicines in front of his waiting clients. He places the mixtures in jars, newspapers, or bottles that have been recycled from the surrounding neighbourhood and then hands them to his customers, along with verbal instructions for their use (see top image Figure 3.1). Julio talks at great length with each group, often oblivious to the growing queue of eager customers around his site. In fact, having the crowd in his garden often provides an opportunity for community education and knowledge transfer, as the nature of an individual's medical issue does not appear to be sensitive or private and other customers often sympathetically share the

View of garden from roof of building across the street

View inside garden

Figure 4.1 Views of the garden

same health concerns and decide to purchase for their own wellbeing the remedy that was recommended to the previous patient. Julio informed me that, in 2015, he consulted with 1,460 people, recording each of their names in a hand-written log along with the remedies and plants he prescribed. The financial transactions are typically conducted in the national currency, the Cuban peso. However, many exchanges also occur through the bartering of goods and services in return for remedies. This fluid and informal economy is typical of a network that involves recycling, inventing, sharing, and creating so as to extend the 'margins of the [...] system' in an economy that somehow finds space in it for all citizens (Figure 1.7).[21]

Julio revealed that all his knowledge of green medicine and religious plants had been gained from the newspaper, television, and radio. So great is his knowledge that he is now a contributor to the sources from which he originally received his education and he now regularly appears on the local radio. During visits, he frequently consulted the resources he kept in a scrapbook of clippings that he stored under the counter so as to validate or confirm his recommendations. His clientele respect his advice and, with little access to the internet or books, they have no better sources. Clearly, Julio is well liked within his community. Passers-by on foot and in bicycle taxis continually shout out greetings to him and often stop to chat or drop off bottles for his use, as containers for medicines, or even plants with which to build future credit. The neighbour across the street invited me up onto his roof several times to see the aerial view of the garden (Figure 4.1). It soon became obvious that the garden is a great source of pride for the neighbourhood as people repeatedly stressed Julio's professionalism and knowledge of plant medicine. The neighbour's roofscape environment was greatly improved by the shade and scents from the vegetation across the street. My host pointed out where Julio lived on the adjacent street in a building that once housed an ice factory. The top floor had recently collapsed, but luckily Julio's unit was on one of the intact lower floors. The neighbour clearly knew all the people in the surrounding houses; he indicated the number of families living in each building and recounted short narratives about each of their life circumstances. Such insight was only possible as the same families have lived within the community since the Revolution. Until recently, the government did not permit house sales and the house swapping system was so cumbersome that people largely remain in place for their lifetime. Later that day, I noticed that the gate of the site was shut, but the lock was not secured. With many eyes on the street and with so much familiarity of people's everyday habits within the neighbourhood, the activity in the garden was always closely monitored.

The site, owned in usufruct by Julio, is approximately 13 x 34 metres (the garden portion is 13 x 24 metres) and consists of ten beds, each 0.75 metres wide, constructed from corrugated siding recycled from collapsed

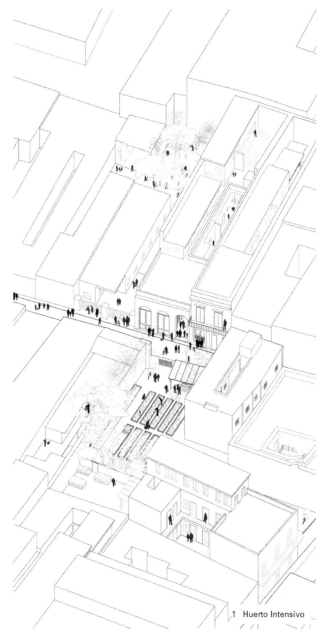

1 Huerto Intensivo

Figure 4.2 Axonometric drawing of the San Isidro neighbourhood

buildings (Figure 4.2). The canopy roof for the transaction counter and the storage shed were also created from found materials within the neighbourhood, including wood studs, steel posts, and corrugated steel siding. The wrought iron gates and grilles survived from when the original house had collapsed. Julio and his assistants work in the garden and periodically schoolchildren help by clearing the paths and beds. Students from four local primary schools regularly come to his site to learn about green medicine. Each school had been named for an important revolutionary: Sergio Luis Ferriol, Carlos Manuel de Cespedes, Don Mariano Mart Navarro, and Oscar Lucero Moya. Each group consisted of 15 to 20 students. They arrived on at the site, after the close of business at 2pm, and sat in the part of the garden Julio called the classroom, situated outside a small makeshift structure he referred to as his office. This small clearing prevented the children from damaging any of the plants as they were briefed on the lessons and afternoon activities, which typically included weeding and watering. Hand-written signs on all of the beds enabled the students to learn the plant names (Figure 4.6). Julio was eager to share his knowledge and so he invited other curious visitors into his garden, ensuring they rubbed powdered chlorine disinfectant on their shoes and hands before entering so as to not contaminate his plants.

Julio's garden and the other activities surrounding it constituted some of the many rhythms of the neighbourhood. Other rhythms were seen surrounding the garbage dumpsters and public telephones which were located adjacent to the site. As many people did not have phones within their homes, they shouted up to friends and family when they received calls. The calls often lasted for over an hour and, at times, when they become heated or emotional, the garbage bins provided some privacy and a place to lean. People also frequently dropped off refuse throughout the day, emptying buckets of organic waste and nylon sacks of dry rubbish. Anything that might be of value to others was placed alongside the dumpsters and people riffled through it for useful *inventar*.

From the garden Julio had an excellent view of the dumpsters and collected items he deemed to be valuable, such as pieces of wood, pots, fixtures, and metal that he observed being discarded. He stockpiled these supplies in organised sections at the rear of his property and used them for ongoing repairs to the site and for trading with the community. As outlined earlier in this book, the government promoted the practice of *inventar*, and recycling was encouraged to reduce garbage. *Inventar* expanded the use of this facility in the community as it was well positioned to collect local discarded items. It served as a central word-of-mouth repository point for this activity as conversations and negotiations were made at this garden to procure different materials for people's construction projects.

Along with the bartering of recycled items, space too was negotiable. At the rear of the property, an adjacent neighbour had carved out a small portion of Julio's usufruct land for hanging up laundry in an outdoor space. As part of a single room within a *solar*, this family acquired, through negotiation, exterior space that doubled their available living area. A flimsy wire mesh fence defined this new boundary. This informal transaction and loss of space did not appear to bother Julio as he reorganised his recycled material storage area to carefully accommodate his neighbour's newly formed outdoor patio.

As the perspective of the street changed, so did its rhythms. From above, on a rooftop, the order of the city blocks and façades became less structured. Amongst the drying clothes, the ruination of the city became even more apparent as the fragile additions and collapses created a precarious roofscape. Viewing the space from above also uncovered the serendipitous opportunities that can occur as a result of a collapse, including access to neighbouring property lines for ventilation, space, or light. This had happened to the north of the site—louvers and windows had been added to the buildings neighbouring the garden to increase cross-ventilation and daylight. However, these collapses challenged the integrity of the adjacent structures. The *solar*, to the south of the garden, has become very compromised due to decay. Heavy rain, hurricanes, and salt air have also taken their toll. Ever resourceful, Julio collected the rainwater that poured from the adjacent roof through a web of gutters and pipes and directed it into barrels along the edge of the property. This symbiotic relationship helped prevent storm water from pooling on the compromised roof, while the access to irrigation water was essential to Julio's operation. Prior to the threat of Hurricane Matthew, in October 2016, Julio and his neighbours cleared debris and leaves from the gutters and pipes in preparation for the downpour.

Along with water and sunlight, compost is the other input required for the garden. Julio used cuttings and household organic matter to produce organic material. To assist with this was a wooden container housing a worm bed and bat guano that acts as a natural fungicide and compost activator. Good compost, according to Julio, was created over a period of three months through the decomposition of organic matter. The high temperatures that accompanied the process brought about chemical and physical changes that produced a fertiliser free from harmful bacteria.[22] Source separation was not officially practiced in Cuban cities but was done informally by Julio. 'On average, the composition of waste from the city of Havana is as follows: paper and cardboard (13.3%); metals (1.8%); plastics (11.0%); glass (2.5%); textiles (2.9%); wood (3.5%); food waste (62.4%); rubber (0.3%); leather (0.5%) and other (2.0%).'[23] Sites of urban agriculture typically acted as the locations for neighbourhood garbage containers, as residents within the community did not want to live adjacent to the odorous bins. They were meant to be emptied daily—although the community was unclear about the exact schedule that appeared to evolve with the specific garbage collection crews. The contents of the bins were sent to the over-flowing landfills at Calle 100, Guanabacoa, and Ocho Vias. Given that the average household produced approximately 65% organic matter, much of this could be composted at urban agricultural farms since they could benefit from organic fertiliser.[24] This already happened informally at Julio's garden and the compost was shared with neighbours and other local producers.

The block surrounding Julio was predominantly residential, interspersed with a few commercial and municipal occupancies. The Office of the Histo-rian's landscaping facility was located across the road, having taken advan-tage of a space where another building had recently collapsed. The crews that worked here tended to the plants within the parks in the Historic Centre. Groups of workers appeared in the early morning and after lunch to collect tools and plants for the day's work. Julio borrowed their tools for use in his garden as he did not have access to a large shovel, rake, or wheelbarrow. He reciprocated this generosity by providing compost for their operation and medicinal plants for their use. There were also a few home-based cafeterias, on the block, where food made in these households' kitchens was served from their doorways to the local people. The owners of the cafeterias on Julio's street purchased oregano and basil from him. Their menus alternated between pizza and a combination of rice, beans, and pork.

Julio's garden is part of multiple networks that include garbage and recycling, water collection, affiliated businesses, the education of children and adults, medical facilities, and a web of neighbourhood stores for daily provisioning (Figure 4.5–Figure 4.8). These stores include the CUC shop and those involved in supplying the subsidised food rationed through the *Libreta de Abastecimiento* (supplies booklet). These include the *bodega* (neighbourhood ration store) and, for meat and eggs, the *carnicería* (meat store). Figure 4.5 shows how provisioning for basic foods is localised over a few blocks in this neighbourhood. Many other administrative and social aspects within Cuban life, in addition to food, also operate at the scale of the block, including the Committee for the Defence of the Revolution (CDR). Approximately three hundred citizens are part of each CDR. The CDRs hold local meetings where concerns between the community and the gov-ernment are discussed. This creates a bottom-up neighbourhood forum to discuss local issues that are organised alongside the state-controlled infra-structure. The CDR was originally designed as a 'neighbourhood watch' in which neighbours surveyed their neighbours and reported any questionable activities. With a democratically elected president, the CDR is currently more involved with organising block parties, local security, community

Figure 4.3 Rhythms and networks across the section, 8am–10am

Figure 4.4 Rhythms and networks across the section, 4pm–6pm

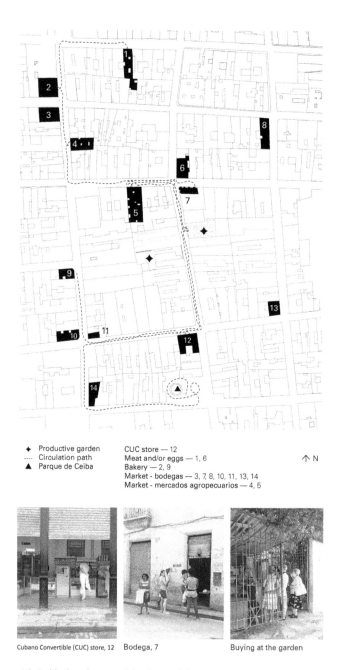

Figure 4.5 Drift showing provisioning activity

healthcare, volunteer work, renovations, festivals, and education than reporting counterrevolutionary activity.[25] Julio was the elected neighbourhood president of the CDR during the study period.

Usufruct access to vacant land or to building materials for repairing one's house is also assessed through the CDR and a request to the Poder Popular (People's Power), the Cuban local government system in charge of distribution. So, while Julio currently has the use of this land, the community in many ways controls the future of his site. Usufruct status requires that the operator, in their use of the land, must contribute to the neighbourhood. These are sites of production and exchange within a community and the usufruct rights to the land dictate that these sites must continually give to the neighbourhood or they risk being reclaimed for alternative uses. Whether the community feels this objective has been adequately accomplished on this land affects whether the tenure is continued. Far from being just a site of production, Julio appeared to be motivated by altruistic incentives and his garden largely operated within the public good; it is not focused solely on providing food and green medicine for economic return but fulfills more pressing needs within the neighbourhood.[26]

In the afternoon and early evening, the street was full of children of every age playing in large groups outside Julio's site. The vegetation in the garden moderated the torrid temperatures making it more comfortable than the neighbouring streets. Chalk, string, and articles of clothing defined the limits of the court or pitch that was continually produced and re-produced. The games that evening included soccer, target practice at cans lined up along Julio's fence, and a game of marbles. These activities were observed by adults on multiple levels in their surrounding homes (decks, roofs, patios, and front steps) and this ensured that these games never became too boisterous. As twilight fell the atmosphere of the street resembled a living room. The doorsteps served as sofas as the community mingled. Chairs were brought into the street to make groupings as drinks were passed around. Voices became quieter as darkness enveloped the community. Lighting largely came from the glow of lamps and televisions inside homes as street lighting was non-existent. Children were sent to bed and the music quietened but the adults remained and talked in hushed tones about everyday issues including baseball, soap operas, work, politics, money, love, and family. One of the most common conversations also involved house sales as Cubans can now legally sell their homes. Hand-written "for sale" signs were starting to appear throughout the neighbourhood. While foreigners are unable to legally purchase property within Cuba, there were whispered discussions within the community about precarious deals taking shape through middle persons or rich Cubans living abroad. As one of the only sites for urban agriculture in the Colonial city, there may be people clamouring for this space.

4.4 Documenting Everyday Life

The intensity of the neighbourhood surrounding the garden in San Isidro required only a few blocks to uncover its diverse networks (Figure 4.2). Walking through the streets revealed many symbiotic goings-on and different actors that included schools and daycares that regularly attended classes at the garden, medical *consultorios* who sent patients to purchase remedies, green pharmacies that dispensed from the site, elderly residents from local care homes who frequented the garden for consultations about health issues; and others who just liked to sit and talk. Likewise, santeros and santeras visited the garden and used plants from it that, according to their faith, targeted specific emotional conflicts, got rid of bad energies, and promoted daily health and happiness.

4.4.1 Drift

Making a series of drift drawings served as an important device for measuring the beats of the city to understand the patterns and shifts in its rhythms.[27] Walking around the streets surrounding the garden highlighted spaces that partake in the everyday life of the community and those that do not. During the study period, I noted the presence of the two economies that separate those with access to hard currency from those without. This was evident in the shops that traded in one economy versus another. The very poorest within the neighbourhood never entered the CUC stores but lingered around the *bodegas*, waiting patiently for new deliveries of goods that were often slow to arrive. Observing these practices revealed patterns. In San Isidro shopping typically occurs daily with each expedition arranged around the household's specific *bodega* and butcher, where the highly subsidised items listed in the Libreta de Abastecimiento (supplies booklet) are available. From there, people obtain bread from the bakery, seasonal fruits and vegetables are purchased from the *agromercado* (market), and herbs from Julio's garden. All of these transactions are in pesos. The local CUC store is visited intermittently for alcohol, juice, or meal variations when money allows. While stocks are often depleted within the peso stores, the proximity is convenient for the staple Cuban meal of rice, beans, and pork—all of which can be obtained within a few blocks of home. Special meals require much more careful planning and access beyond these local networks.

Julio's garden is also actively part of religious practices and healthcare procurement in the community. While spiritual traditions largely take place within homes behind closed doors, the garden sells many of the plants and herbs used in the ceremonies. For medical purposes, the garden is often visited after a trip to the local *consultorio*, followed by a disappointing visit to the pharmacy with no available stock of the prescribed drug, and finally the patient settling on green medicine from the garden (Figure 4.7).

All these many interconnected networks and rhythms converge on the garden—it serves as a hub in the community. When all these activities were combined into a map, the extent of the local networks became clear. Education, food, worship, and healthcare all surround the garden. From these seemingly disparate activities, a point of intensity can be seen where people come together to learn, provision, dispose, and find treatments and hope. The extent of the game-board is approximately eight city blocks (two by four)—a small area where quotidian life within the community unfolds—creating a game-board of symbiotic activity, centred around the garden (Figure 4.5–Figure 4.8).

4.4.2 *Game-Board*

The garden in San Isidro cannot be understood in isolation or at only one moment in time. It is a game-board of symbiotic relationships where the different actors have reciprocal interactions in and around this vegetated clearing in the city. Both human and ecological connections are visible beyond the decorative metal gates in the façades of the buildings surrounding the site. Deeper penetration into the block discloses different rhythms that are not visible from the street. Within the courtyards of the *solares* that surrounded the garden, whole families live within a single room in homes that spill out into a collective courtyard (Figure 4.3 and Figure 4.4). Residents on all sides encroach on the garden, with a window or a fence claiming a small part of the site. Vents, openings, and make-shift structures trespass as the occupants make informal claims to appropriate space, light, and ventilation. The garden provides a cool and fragrant sanctuary within this hot and humid city.

These game-board activities surrounding Julio's garden change throughout the day and include

- The community recycles glass and plastic bottles by pushing them through the fence of the garden rather than disposing of them in the garbage. Julio uses these to dispense the plant remedies from the garden (Figure 3.1 top image).
- The Office of the Historian's garden, across the street, shares tools, seedlings, and labourers with the site while Julio supplies them with medicinal plants and compost.
- The sale of medicinal plants helps alleviate the scarcity of allopathic medication shortages at the pharmacies.

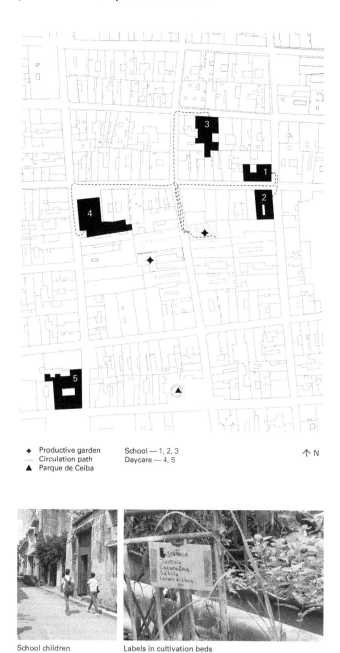

Figure 4.6 Drift of school children and their interaction with the garden

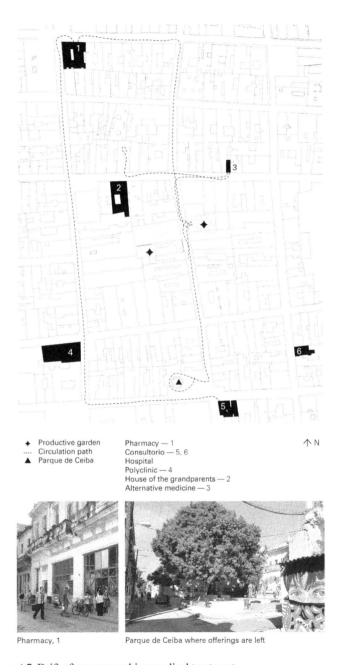

✦ Productive garden	Pharmacy — 1	↑ N
···· Circulation path	Consultorio — 5, 6	
▲ Parque de Ceiba	Hospital	
	Polyclinic — 4	
	House of the grandparents — 2	
	Alternative medicine — 3	

Pharmacy, 1   Parque de Ceiba where offerings are left

Figure 4.7 Drift of persons seeking medical treatment

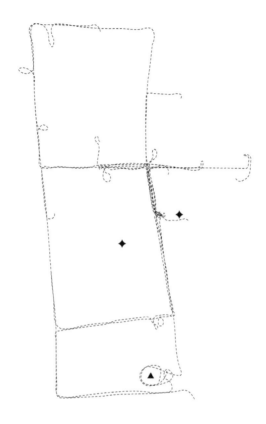

Waiting for medical or spiritual advice at the garden

Figure 4.8 Combined drift activities

- The collection of water from the neighbours' roofs is used for irrigation. The collection of this water reduces the amount of storm water that pours into the streets.
- Knowledge, teaching, and education are exchanged with school children and the community. In turn, the gardeners learn from their informed customers about the plants they need in order to perform Santería rituals for the various orishas.
- Conviviality is very apparent amongst customers, passers by, neighbours, assistants, and producers.
- Children play while adults sit in the shade the trees in the garden cast on the street.
- Other businesses, especially mobile carts, collect around this garden, thereby creating a hub for commerce in the neighbourhood.

4.4.3 Layering

Studying these sites revealed both quantitative and qualitative layers of data. From the Plan Maestro's office, it was possible to get information about the age of the buildings, the population density living in each block, and the state of the structures (Figure 2.1).[28] Visual inspections of the buildings surrounding the site revealed different layers of decay and collapse that may happen over time (Figure 4.10). If there is no intervention, the future unabated deterioration in this neighbourhood will bring about the profound loss of structures within the community. Many citizens live in constant fear of collapse, this only intensifies when the city experiences heavy rain and storms.

Other layers that were important to study included the weather and how it shapes buildings. The climate is part of quotidian life in Havana. It is also one of the most important rhythms to affect the city. It includes the intensity of the sun during the summer, the strength of the rain, and the fear and devastation of hurricanes in the autumn months. These climatic events shape everyday life and the city's architecture. Research by Abel Tablada highlighted some of the best practices for building in a tropical climate. Such strategies include the incorporation of voids within both the plans and in the cross sections of buildings in the city.[29] These absences of space take the form of courtyards and smaller ventilation shafts (*traspatios*) and collectively they promote air flow. These voids are open at the top while the main courtyards have wide entrances (*zaguán*) to allow for both ventilation and direct connection to the street, thereby allowing people access into the building. The inter-connection of all these courtyards is important to providing air circulation. Everyday life unfolds within these courtyards—in this layer of absence. In fact, in buildings where the ratio of open space (courtyards and shafts) meet or exceed the mandated 15% of a building's footprint, the quality of life within their cramped *solares* seems to have improved compared to other buildings. This layer of absence provides space to grow plants, hang laundry, and sit outside. And it was common to find vegetation in these spaces where this growth simultaneously delighted the senses, eased tension, provided food, and cooled the space. Indeed, plants reduce the urban-heat-island effect as vegetated areas absorb less heat than the surrounding impervious surfaces do, resulting in noticeable differences in temperature. In addition, the water released into the atmosphere through the process of transpiration cools surface temperatures through evaporation.

The layer of collapse across the community motivated the occupants of neighbouring buildings to modify or add informal openings and fenestration to increase the cross ventilation in their homes. Windows with louvers were constructed to provide shade from the sun. Makeshift solar shading structures appear to reduce the exposure to direct sunlight. Vegetation growing on multiple floors and on trellises also added shade and plants. All these layers surrounding the garden embody the specificity of the community.

4.4.4 Rhizome

This study looked for rhizomatic relationships—combinations of characteristics that are seemingly unrelated—yet are inextricably linked. Garbage removal and building collapse, two seemingly unconnected criteria, are related within this decaying city (Figure 4.11). Garbage is collected next to sites of urban agriculture, as people do not want it adjacent to their homes due to the smell and mess. Recorded over time, a series of photographs of this garden in San Isidro shows much about life in this city. The number of garbage containers has increased, along with the quantity of the garbage, every year since 2013. This suggests the population has access to more commodities, or possibly, garbage collection is less frequent. The make-up of the garbage has differed over time. It has increasingly consisted of more construction materials from the decaying buildings and also packaging material, such as cardboard and styrofoam. The care with which the garbage is collected also evolved. In 2013, garbage was picked up by hand; later it was picked up with front-end loaders that could hardly fit through the narrow streets. As they moved back and forth and swung their buckets, they hit buildings, thereby increasing the possibility of damage and collapse. The final remnants of garbage used to be swept up with brooms to leave the street clean. This no longer happens, and the residue persists in the streets. The number of people scavenging through the garbage has also increased as the quantity and usefulness of the discarded materials has improved. Photographs taken over a six-year period show all these patterns. The garbage bins have increased in number, but they nevertheless continually overflow.

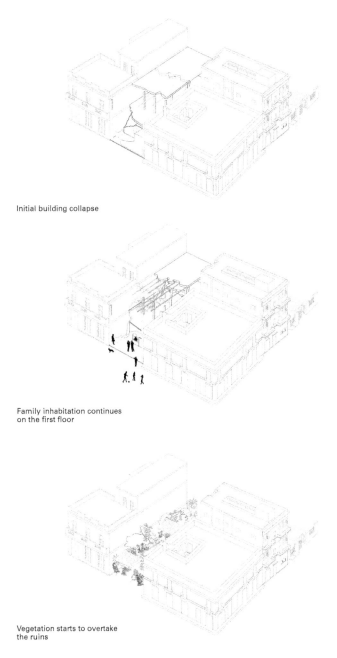

Initial building collapse

Family inhabitation continues
on the first floor

Vegetation starts to overtake
the ruins

Figure 4.9 Rhythms of collapse over time in San Isidro

Current state of collapses

Predicted future collapses if construction issues are not alleviated

Figure 4.10 Layers of predicted collapse over time in San Isidro

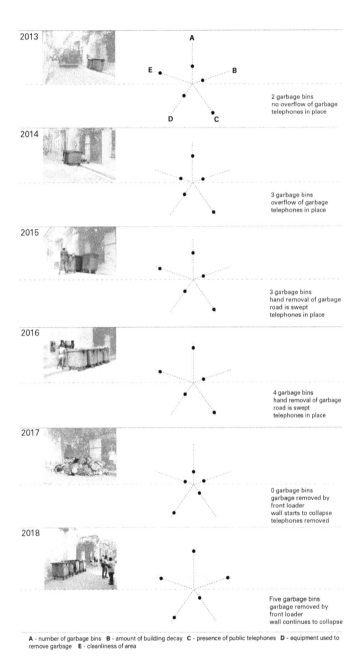

2013
A
E
B
D
C
2 garbage bins
no overflow of garbage
telephones in place

2014
3 garbage bins
overflow of garbage
telephones in place

2015
3 garbage bins
hand removal of garbage
road is swept
telephones in place

2016
4 garbage bins
hand removal of garbage
road is swept
telephones in place

2017
0 garbage bins
garbage removed by
front loader
wall starts to collapse
telephones removed

2018
Five garbage bins
garbage removed by
front loader
wall continues to collapse

A - number of garbage bins   B - amount of building decay   C - presence of public telephones   D - equipment used to remove garbage   E - cleanliness of area

Figure 4.11 Rhizome: state of garbage and decay over a six-year period

In 2017, they disappeared altogether, and the garbage lay in disarray. By 2018, Julio's garden wall along the street had been partially destroyed as the garbage removal increased the amount of building decay.

At the garden site, the collection of recyclable materials had also increased over the last two years of the study period, along with this increase in garbage—as people are seeing the usefulness of what is being discarded. Electing to use valuable space in the garden for the storage of this resource indicates that it is an important commodity. This is because construction materials are a continual dilemma within Cuba. The scarcity is a partial consequence of the enduring embargo, as it jeopardises imports, while government-owned companies that are associated with material production suffer from the rampant theft of products. Poorly paid workers and weak control mechanisms have led to the clandestine transfer to the black market of these limited and valuable products, such as steel, rebar, electrical and telephone cables, aggregates, and cement, all of which are vital to contractors.[30] The use of existing and recycled materials help to counteract the scarcity and the challenges that are also imposed by trade isolation and shortages.

After a substantial collapse, the process of clean-up has evolved over the years of the study. At the start of this research, the state cleaned a site up quickly and efficiently. Onlookers and taking photographs of a collapse were prohibited, and within weeks of a collapse, a masonry street wall was constructed to conceal the hole in the city. This was an embarrassment to be hidden by the state. These sites were then used for temporary occupancies, including the storage of bici-taxis, markets, or gardens. Now, the process is less precise and there is less state intervention (Figure 4.9). The dead are still taken away and the injured are triaged. Dangerous items may be removed. If the damage is extensive, then the residents will never return to the property. Often a collapse will spill out onto the street and traffic and pedestrians are diverted (Figure 1.6). A temporary and flimsy hoarding fence may be erected. Then there is an extended period for scavenging the debris. Experienced and entrepreneurial self-employed contractors immediately arrive on site to acquire any intact masonry blocks and valuable materials, particularly wood elements such as doors or banisters for their clients' construction projects. In fact, there is a growing market for pre-ordering artefacts from sites of future collapse, through salvaging contractors. The next wave of scavengers is generally less purposeful and mainly opportunistic. This garden is part of this second wave. Here raw materials such as wood and metal are picked out of the decay. Others take the rubble and pulverise it into aggregate for mixing with cement to make concrete or to construct homemade blocks. After several weeks, thoroughly picked through, the site just sits in a state of ruin and the community uses it as an extended garbage dump. It often remains in this condition for several years, until the government's demolition team finally arrives with its heavy machinery and clears it away; the debris is then sent to overflowing landfills. At several stages of this process, the entrepreneurial activities that emerge from this tragedy lesson the burden on the environment. What used to be a procedure entirely controlled by the state is now part of an evolving economy.

Prior to an imminent collapse, the authorities often send out repeated warnings to vacate dangerous buildings or homeowners try to prop up their homes at risk of collapse. Introducing scaffolding to the site at this stage enables some of the existing and surrounding buildings to safely remain intact while people continue to live within the space (see Figure 4.9). Shoring is constructed from materials, such as wood, steel rebar, or bamboo and Julio is able to supply some of these materials. The scaffolding remains in place for so long that it is eventually incorporated into temporary informal dwellings that appear on such sites as the provisional becomes the permanent. Figure 4.12 shows a catalogue of recycled materials observed while on a walk through the streets of San Isidro. The commonest components are rebar, dimensional lumber, aggregates, and many pieces of mismatched masonry (stone, concrete, and brick).

4.5 Conclusion

This garden site in San Isidro is proto-typical of the neighbourhood as there are many comparable sites of collapse. Figure 4.10 shows the extent of ruination that is evident in La Habana Vieja and where future collapses are predicted. Two other decayed buildings are in the same block as Julio's garden. Without structural intervention, another two buildings will fall for a total of four within this single block. This site is part of the evolving rhythms of a neighbourhood that includes more decay than regeneration.

Currently the players and programmes in the game-board around the garden in San Isidro include different levels of interaction around the site. The most regular rhythmic relationships with the site include the everyday comings and goings. These consist of the producer and workers that engage with the garden every day. The next level includes the groups that consistently come to the site: the regular clientele who seek medications; students from the school who attend weekly classes; the elderly from the *casa de los abuelos* (daycare for the elderly), who are walking around the block for exercise; the Santería practitioners in search of specific plants for rituals and healing; and the staff from the Historians Office with its reciprocal relationship with the garden through tools, labourers, compost, plants, and seedlings. The next tier of interaction includes the services, businesses, and networks that engage with the site, including the doctors who send patients to the garden, the pharmacies that prescribe the products, and people involved with the

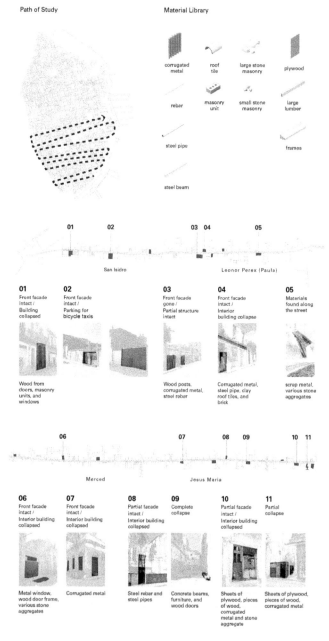

Figure 4.12 Chris Sahagun: catalogue of building materials, 2018

Graphics by Stavros Kondeas, Rita Wang, Alicia McDowell (Gilmore), and Lucas McDowell

informal recycling of bottles passed through Julio's fence, and the disposing of organics for compost.

Beyond this interaction, the surrounding community operates in multiple ways. Competing priorities come into play with the continuous need for housing as people, both temporarily and permanently, are displaced by the decaying and collapsing accommodations in the surrounding community. As the land of the garden is owned in usufruct, this means that the tenure of that land is precarious. Space and land are in short supply. However, the altruistic contributions of this garden to the community help to secure its ongoing tenancy. Conviviality, generosity, and an evolving contribution to the people are important characteristics to ensure the continued occupancy of Julio and his garden.

Several forms of urbanism coexist in San Isidro. Unlike most other Latin American cities where the formal and informal are confined to different and often gated parts of the city, within Havana these multiple worlds occupy the same space. The buildings of crumbling masonry, concrete, and steel form the skeleton of the everyday kinetic city that is made and re-made within these decaying structures and the adjacent streets. The temporal occupation of this space shows resilience and ingenuity and demonstrates 'how spatial limits' can be 'expanded to include formally unimagined uses in dense urban conditions'.[31] Julio's garden and the surrounding neighbourhood display cooperation, creativity, and resourcefulness as they adapt to everyday struggles. Relationships stitch together the fragile built environment as resources of land, water, shade, waste, ventilation, and crops are shared and redistributed in a type of community sustainability and symbiosis.

Visiting the same site at different times of the day and night and during different seasons revealed the qualities and atmospheres of the place, the intricate life that unfolded daily, the intimacy, conviviality, and specificity of the block. Rhythmanalysis served as a type of urban ethnography that untangled the complexity of people's actions into definable beats to create a collective *oeuvre* of everyday life.[32] As these spaces are controlled and constrained by structures, systems, nature, and time tables within the urban environment, so it is possible to study and categorise their rhythmicity into 'everyday social routines, patterns of movement . . . sensory practices, circadian and seasonal cycles of nature'.[33] The drawings show how we can uncover the performative, experiential, and sensorial qualities of urban life rather than focusing only on the visual and formal. These ordinary spaces are neither explicitly public nor private but rather provide a place for interactions to occur where things are cultivated, made, mixed, considered, and sold in a space that is made and re-made throughout the day, week, and year. Figures 4.3 and 4.4 show how the space is occupied throughout a day, with the clock indicating precise times when activities occur. These drawings demonstrate how borders to this site are shared and how work, knowledge, and conviviality are exchanged. There is a subtlety to these activities and this is only revealed through interaction. Much can be learned from going into this neighbourhood and listening carefully to its rhythms. This required continual visits, engagement with the people, and comprehending the nuances and networks of the place. Understanding these rhythmic attributes may hold far more promise for the future city than the morphology and typology the architect typically uses to measure a city, or the economic and political indicators the economist usually uses to quantify the success of our cities. Change within cities is inevitable and Havana will collapse if it does not evolve. But in many ways, it seems as though many of the answers already exist within the community in the everyday habits that are continually evolving to construct a spatiality that is robust, flexible, entrepreneurial, and sustainable. These polyrhythmic layers include the natural, cultural, and social in a resilient ecology that includes people and their everyday activities within this rhythmic study of San Isidro in La Habana Vieja.

Notes

1. Smith and Hetherington, "Urban Rhythms: Mobilities, Space and Interaction in the Contemporary City," 5.
2. Neil Smith, "New Globalism, New Urbanism: Gentrification as Global Urban Strategy," *Antipode* 34, no. 3 (2002): 436.
3. Smith and Hetherington, "Urban Rhythms: Mobilities, Space and Interaction in the Contemporary City," 5.
4. Louis Wirth, "Urbanism as a Way of Life," *American Journal of Sociology* 44, no. 1 (1938): 1–24.
5. Highmore, *Cityscapes: Cultural Readings in the Material and Symbolic City*, 145–146.
6. Amin and Thrift, *Cities: Reimagining the Urban*, 19.
7. Lefebvre, *Rhythmanalysis: Space, Time and Everyday Life*, 27.
8. Tiwari, "Being a Rhythm Analyst in the City of Varanasi," 292.
9. Hernández, Kellett and Allen, *Rethinking the Informal City: Critical Perspectives from Latin America*, xi. Foreword by Rahul Mehrotra.
10. Smith and Hetherington, "Urban Rhythms: Mobilities, Space and Interaction in the Contemporary City," 6.
11. de Certeau, *The Practice of Everyday Life*, 91–110.
12. City Population, "City Population," www.citypopulation.de/en/cuba/admin/ (accessed April 2021).
13. Taylor, *Inside El Barrio: A Bottom-Up View of Neighborhood Life in Castro's Cuba*, 149.
14. Taylor, *Inside El Barrio: A Bottom-Up View of Neighborhood Life in Castro's Cuba*, 150
15. Gisela Díaz, Ana Ma. de la Peña and Alfonso Alfonso, "Learning from the Past: The Traditional Compact City in Hot-Humid Climates" (PLEA 2006: The 23rd

Conference on Passive and Low Energy Architecture, Geneva, Switzerland, September 6–8, 2006.
16. A. Tablada et al., "On Natural Ventilation and Thermal Comfort in Compact Urban Environments: The Old Havana Case," *Building and Environment* 44, no. 9 (2009): 1943.
17. Scarpaci, Segre and Coyula, *Havana: Two Faces of the Antillean Metropolis*, 105.
18. Mario Coyula and Jill Hamberg, *Understanding Slums: The Case of Havana, Cuba* (Cambridge: David Rockefeller Center for Latin American Studies, 2004), 28.
19. Luisa Iñiguez, *Las Tantas Habanas: Estrategias Para Comprender Sus Dinámicas Sociales* (La Habana: Editorial UH, 2014), 55.
20. City Population, "City Population".
21. Hernández, Kellett and Allen, *Rethinking the Informal City: Critical Perspectives from Latin America*, xiii. Foreword by Rahul Mehrotra.
22. Koont, *Sustainable Urban Agriculture in Cuba*, 92.
23. Ma Espinosa Lloréns et al., "Characterization of Municipal Solid Waste from the Main Landfills of Havana City," *Waste Management* 28, no. 10 (2008): 2017.
24. I. Körner, I. Saborit-Sánchez and Y. Aguilera-Corrales, "Proposal for the Integration of Decentralised Composting of the Organic Fraction of Municipal Solid Waste into the Waste Management System of Cuba," *Waste Management* 28, no. 1 (2008): 64–72.
25. Taylor, *Inside El Barrio: A Bottom-Up View of Neighborhood Life in Castro's Cuba*, 81–82.
26. Gold, "Urban Gardens: Private Property or the Ultimate Socialist Experience?," 33.
27. McDonough, "Situationist Space," 65.
28. Plan Maestro, "Oficina Del Historiador De La Ciudad De La Habana," www.planmaestro.ohc.cu/
29. Tablada et al., "On Natural Ventilation and Thermal Comfort in Compact Urban Environments: The Old Havana Case," 1957.
30. Rojas Osmar Laffita, "Materiales De Construcción, Ese Delicado Asunto: La Corrupción Mina Toda La Industria," *Cubanet*, www.cubanet.org/actualidad-destacados/materiales-de-construccion-ese-delicado-asunto/ (accessed January 2018).
31. Hernández, Kellett and Allen, *Rethinking the Informal City: Critical Perspectives from Latin America*, xii. Foreword by Rahul Mehrotra.
32. Panu Lehtovuori and Hille Koskela, "From Momentary to Historic: Rhythms in the Social Production of Urban Space, the Case of Calçada De Sant'Ana, Lisbon," *Sociological Review* 61 (2013): 124–143.
33. Wunderlich, "Place-Temporality and Rhythmicity: A New Aesthetic and Methodological Foundation for Urban Design Theory and Practice," 63–64.

5 Living Together in Cayo Hueso

5.1 Background

By the end of the sixteenth century, the expanding town of San Cristóbal de la Habana needed access to the surrounding hinterlands for sustenance to feed its burgeoning population and raw materials to build much needed infrastructure. Roads such as Monte, Reina, and San Lázaro connected the centre to agricultural lands, quarries, and forests, while the Zanja Real (Royal canal) carried water from the Almendares River to the port.[1] In 1674, the construction of a wall around San Cristóbal de La Habana was an important step to help distinguish it as a city rather than just a town. It was completed in 1797, but as the population continued to grow, it became necessary to expand beyond the wall and the municipality of Centro Habana became one of the city's first extramural suburbs.[2] The present municipality is demarcated to the north by the Strait of Florida, to the south by the municipality of Cerro, to the east by La Habana Vieja, and to the west lies the municipality of Plaza de la Revolución (Figure 1.3). Centro Habana is one of Havana's oldest municipalities. It was finally registered as part of the city in 1912. Between 1919 and 1943, the population increased substantially and, despite governmental efforts to curtail this growth, it has continued to remain high even with its profound loss of housing stock.[3]

Cuba was finally liberated from Spain after the Spanish War of Independence, in 1898, but the United States continued to occupy the country. Even after Cuba formally gained independence from the USA in 1902, the economic and cultural presence of the Americans continued. The USA invested money in La Habana's infrastructure and developed Vedado and Miramar as elegant residential neighbourhoods. The rich left the centre for the wide streets, gardens, and parks of these new suburbs, making room for the low-income seasonal workers employed in construction, tobacco factories, or at the dockyards. These workers were domiciled in rooming houses in sub-divided mansions (*cuarterías)* and in rooms surrounding a central courtyard (*ciudadelas)* situated in La Habana Vieja and Centro Habana,

DOI: 10.4324/9781003201410-5

where densities steadily increased.[4] The remaining residents were poor and predominantly black, a demographic that remains today. Out of this racial segregation, a new type of socio-economic seclusion has evolved as fewer Afro-Cubans work within a tourist sector that provides some of the highest incomes earned by people who live within the city.

Centro Habana is the most densely populated of the 15 municipalities that make up La Habana,[5] with approximately 133,110 inhabitants living within 3.5 square kilometres.[6] This concentration may be substantially higher due to overcrowding and the precarious living conditions.[7] In addition, Centro Habana has very few green areas or public spaces and the urban agriculture sites and Parque de Trillo are the only accessible vegetated spaces in the community. The building stock is deteriorated, due to the age of the housing and the lack of maintenance. Bathrooms and laundry facilities are often located in the courtyards and shared among multiple households. The occupation of the blocks is high and the mandated 15% of free ventilation areas in building plans is rarely maintained as these are often infilled with the informal construction of lofts and additions (Figure 5.2).[8] Along with the irregular water supply, the wastewater system is dilapidated, the refuse collection is inefficient, and aged vehicles and local industries in-between dwelling spaces produce high levels of pollution. Centro Habana has the highest rate of building decay in the country with '70% of the houses classified by the Municipal Department of Housing as bad [and] 38% [are] uninhabitable'.[9] Cayo Hueso is in the north-west area of the municipality and occupies less than one square kilometre.[10]

5.2 The Community

Cayo Hueso means 'bone key'. In this community there are many followers of the Afro-Cuban religions of Santería and Palo Monte. The name Cayo Hueso is thought to have a deep significance for the neighbourhood. In reality, it was probably adopted by migrants from Key West, Florida, as *hueso* sounds similar to the word 'west'.[11] In the early 1970s, highly decayed buildings in Cayo Hueso were demolished to make way for urban renewal projects that included prefabricated walk-ups and high-rise apartments. These projects have been largely unsuccessful as the buildings were poorly constructed and they do not engage with street life within the neighbourhood. In 1988, the Grupo para el Desarrollo Integral de la Capital (Group for the Comprehensive Development of the City) set up Talleres de Transformación Integral del Barrio (Neighbourhood Transformation Workshops) in areas with urgent needs, including Cayo Hueso, Atarés, and La Güinera.[12] These workshops took stock of 'the buildings, infrastructure, green spaces, and amenities, and identified social, economic and environmental problems,

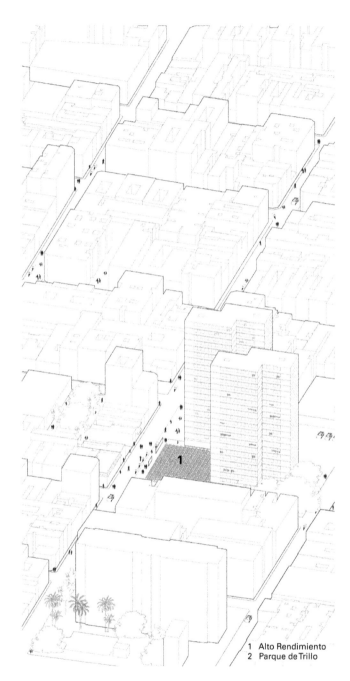

1 Alto Rendimiento
2 Parque de Trillo

Figure 5.1 Axonometric drawing of the Cayo Hueso neighbourhood

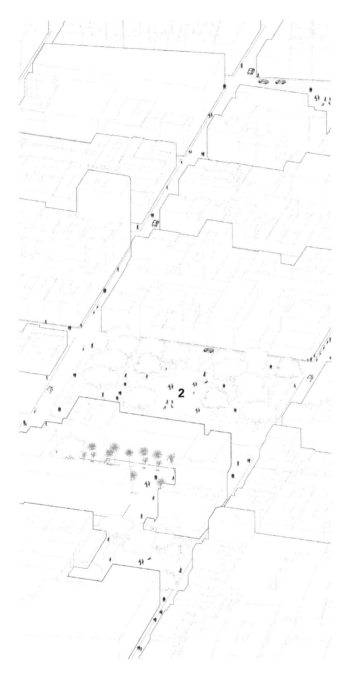

Figure 5.1 (Continued)

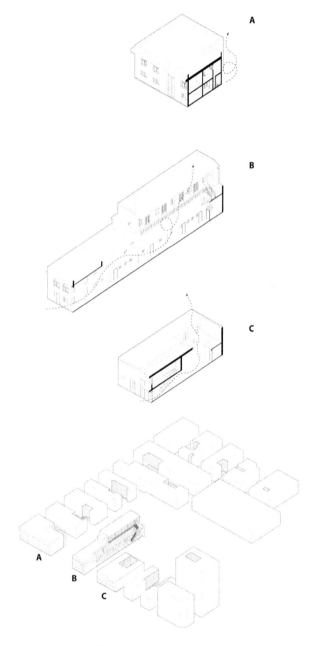

Figure 5.2 Morphology of Cayo Hueso and ventilation strategy

including those related to housing, education, healthcare, food supply and pollution'.[13] Leveraging local resources and labour, the workshops were led by multi-disciplinary teams that included architects, engineers, sociologists, and social workers. Collectively they implemented neighbourhood initiatives.[14] Successful community programmes included the creation of recreation spaces and events, the construction of community gardens, and the repair of decayed buildings. As part of this, the Parque de Trillo hosts diverse social and fitness activities for all age groups with the exact endeavour determined by the intensity of the sun. Shady mornings facilitated the space being used for exercise classes, while in the evenings, soccer games occurred. One morning, a group of women with wooden boxes partook in a step class led by an energetic male teacher, another morning a Tai Chi class occurred, mainly consisting of older participants. Encouraged by the state, community fitness is gaining in popularity. In addition to recreation, the park also holds much spiritual significance, with ceiba trees at each corner. White ribbons adorn their branches while plastic bags full of food offerings are left beside their trunks (Figure 1.8).

In 2016, Wi-Fi was installed in the park as something for social engagement rather than for private entertainment or work. Wi-Fi cards produced by Empresa de Telecomunicaciones de Cuba S.A. (ETECSA) were sold for two CUCs at a booth across the road in a desolate site where a building had collapsed several years before. Benches were spread throughout this lot, but during the day no one sat on them due to the lack of shade. Everybody purchased their cards and made their way across the road to the park. Single people and groups spread throughout the park, under the canopy of trees, to connect to the internet; two CUCs per card allowed for one hour of access so this is an expensive pursuit for the average Cuban. However, the cost was substantially less than the 10 CUCs it was in 2015. Family groups gathered around devices, talking loudly to distant relatives and jostling for space on their tiny screens.

5.3 The Garden

One of the only other vegetated spaces in the community is the Organopónico de Alto Rendimiento (also called U.E.B. Centro Rachel Pérez), which is a site of urban agriculture. The head producer informed me that the site produced between 15 and 20 kilograms of vegetables and medicinal plants per square metre of cultivation space each year. Several separately owned and operated businesses are attached to the garden, including a butcher, a fruit juice stand, a preservative maker and seller, an ornamental plant store, and a technical agriculture consultant (CTA). The CTA gives free horticultural advice to customers and sells seedlings and supplies for cultivation in backyards and patios. Close to this site, another group of neighbours converted an apartment building's central courtyard into a banana plantation, and they share the harvest with the building's occupants and sell the excess at the adjacent market.

This garden (Figures 5.1 and 5.3) is located in the shade of two imposing and dilapidated residential towers—this site demonstrates the spatial paradoxes that exist within this country. On the one hand, Cuba has initiated nationwide infrastructure to serve leading healthcare research and delivery. Formal education is offered by the state to support the local practice of urban agriculture. On the other hand, the current reality is that the country has declining access to medical supplies and the population has had to increasingly rely on informally procured homeopathic alternatives. In addition, this farming site matches the United Nation's definitions of informality as the cultivators lack security of tenure and the land occupies an abandoned space in-between overcrowded and collapsing buildings. The producers have limited access to water and sanitation for their operations, the beds and structures are constructed from found and somewhat dangerous materials (such as asbestos tiles), and the garden is situated next to overflowing garbage collection points.[15] Despite all this, the space fills a void in food and healthcare delivery in the city as the production of green medicine increasingly helps mitigate the scarcity of conventional medicine. The site also exhibits entrepreneurialism, a creative and ecological resourcefulness, in a country where such practices are becoming the vanguard of the economy.[16] It also facilitates serendipitous interactions between diverse individuals as work, knowledge, goods, and conviviality are exchanged. The producers within these gardens demonstrate ingenuity and resilience, akin to Lévi-Strauss's bricoleur, whose

> universe is closed and the rules of his game are always to make do with 'whatever is at hand', that is to say with a set of tools and materials which is always finite and is also heterogeneous because what it contains bears no relation to the current project, or indeed to any project, but is the contingent result of all the occasions there have been to renew or enrich the stock or to maintain it with the remains of previous constructions or destructions.[17]

As drawings Figures 5.4 and 5.5 show, this 'universe' includes the community and the networks, surrounding the site, that flow into and around the garden throughout the day and year and include social, economic, and ecological rhythms.

This garden occupies the corner of two streets—José de San Martin and Espada—a corner site flanked by two 21-storey high-rise towers, named

Figure 5.3 View from inside the garden

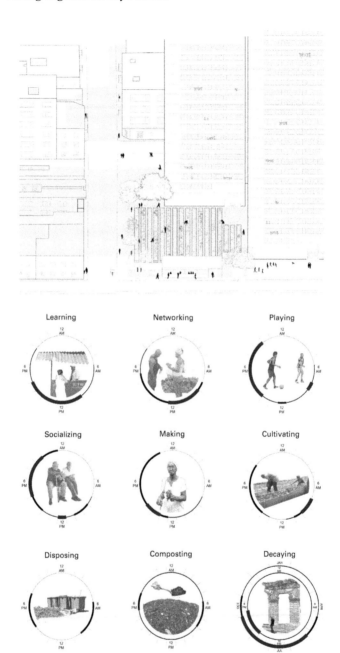

Figure 5.4 Rhythms and networks across the section, 8am–10am

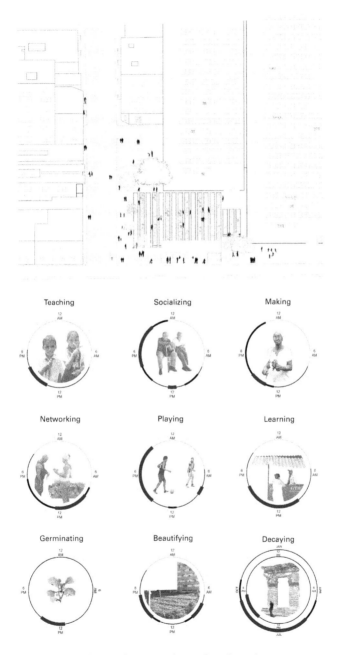

Figure 5.5 Rhythms and networks across the section, 4pm–6pm

Edificio Rachel Pérez and Edificio San José. These towers were built in the 1980s and are now prematurely decayed from the assault of salt air and storms. Rebar protrudes from the precast concrete panels, and it is only a matter of time before there is a major failure. Washing hangs from the windows and frequently falls into the garden—maybe as a precursor to the possible future collapse of the whole structure. At times, the south-east tower casts much needed shadow across the garden and its plants and workers. However, these tall buildings also create wind patterns that the farmers say burn the plants. An overgrown chain-link fence surrounds the perimeter of the garden and, along with the dumpsters adjacent to the site, makes it difficult to see the garden from the street.

Conversations with José, the head producer, revealed that he started operating the garden in 2003. After the scarcity of the 1990s, he had a strong desire to have more control over his food security. An opportunity presented itself when this land was made available for cultivation. As he lived in one of the adjacent towers, it was easy for him to run the facility. Originally trained as a food scientist, José received tuition in farming and obtained supplies including soil and seeds from the Ministry of Agriculture. It was obvious he enjoyed working on this land. He told me, with pleasure and excitement, that every day of the week, he works there from 6am until 5pm.Two or three other employees assist him from 8am to 5pm but they also have other state employment, and their hours were dependent upon their other activities. In fact, while I was there it was often hard to distinguish the workers from the friends and customers who dropped into the site, sometimes to help, sit and chat, or pick up or drop off supplies (Figure 1.9). José informed me that the facility receives daily deliveries because it is part of a larger cooperative that includes farmland in the Municipality of Guanabacoa. The sale of produce from these other locations has enabled them to expand their offerings through their association with this larger farm.

The garden specialises in growing lettuce, spinach, broccoli, and onions. In addition, medicinal plants are produced including aloe vera, moringa, marjoram, hibiscus, and cilantro. The garden's aloe vera is renowned throughout the province. These plants are important to Afro-Cuban religious ceremonies and for different types of green medicine. In 2009 and 2015, the Ministerio de Salud Pública sanctioned many forms of alternative treatment through Ministry of Public Health Laws 261 and 381, making sites of urban agriculture an integral part of the country's healthcare system. These laws incorporated criteria surrounding the teaching, medical care, and scientific research of these therapies into the mainstream health service and the universities' curricula. While the use of these treatments had already been prevalent within different cultural groups, sanctioning their use as viable treatments has helped relieve the overtaxed health service of the burden of providing all the country's healthcare needs. It has also validated these everyday practices and made them mainstream. The types of natural and traditional medicines that have been approved by the Resolución include those related to phytotherapy (plant-derived medications) and apitherapy (bee-derived products), as well as traditional Asian therapeutic exercise, acupuncture, homeopathy, Floral Therapy, and the Bach Flower Remedy System (a health system based upon 38 plants).[18] These practices are not considered alternative treatments outside the state health system but are concurrently used by many of the same physicians. The use of plants in Santería is not officially sanctioned by the state. The explanation given to me was that Santería is grounded in traditional cultural knowledge that is passed on generationally and orally, while the other practices are studied as a science at institutions of higher learning, but ultimately similar treatments are recommended in both practices.[19] Many of these activities were supported by this site. Furthermore, the producers informed me that they grew custom orders, including special order plants from seedlings or from plants that are supplied by the client, doctor, or pharmacy across the road.

The medicinal use of plants has had a long tradition in Cuba. The plants used by santeros and santeras are for the treatment of physical and psychological disorders and spiritual and ritual use. Santería is considered a practical religion that encourages balance within the world. *Aché*, or the spiritual energy present in the universe, is central to all Santería practices. Practitioners hope to acquire more *aché* and maintain it through ethical behaviours and by paying attention to spiritual matters. Certain plants are believed to possess *aché*, the power to 'heal disease and to promote happiness and wellbeing'.[20] Wild-growing *egwes* (plants, herbs, and weeds used in Santería) are reputed to possess greater power for healing than those purchased in a store. While not the ideal situation, allowing people to pick their own plants in the garden in Centro is thought to increase the plants' potency over pre-cut, store-bought products. Nervous disorders, muscle pains, headaches, cancer, and fevers are all believed to be treatable, in some capacity, through *aché*. Practitioners wander throughout the garden's beds and carefully consider the options for their 'ozains and omieros', which 'are the two main classes of plant concoctions used'.[21] The beds within the garden are 1.15 metres in width and are mainly constructed from asbestos board supported by rebar stakes. Irrigation tubes snake between the plantings. With 0.6 metres between the beds, it is relatively easy to walk in-between them, to view the plant species and to lean over and pick the selected items.

This site is simultaneously a pharmacy, a market, and a place to gossip. Shoppers often spend 15 minutes or more at each of the adjacent kiosks, chatting with the owners about their wares, before possibly making a purchase. The technical agriculture consultant (CTA) is a paid government employee and clients often discuss their horticultural issues with this person for over half an hour or longer. At the juice stand, beverages are served in glass cups, and this requires that the consumer stand by the counter and converse while they drink their beverages. Sometimes they wander to the other outlets or into the garden, always returning the glass. In fact, the entryway into the garden serves as both a market and a public space. Shaded from the intense sun, the customer is invited in to purchase pre-picked produce, items brought in from the partner farms, or to sit and rest for a moment. This is particularly important as the east–west orientation of this street makes the sun particularly forbidding, particularly around noon when it is high in the sky. During the day, a group of people are always gathered in the shade of the market entryway, including workers, friends, family, and shoppers. Customers walk through this space and into the garden to pick their own produce or wait while the workers bring it to them while they wait out of the sun.

This covered workspace operates as a social space and a living room. At most hours of the day, during the week and on the weekends, people can be seen both working and relaxing in this space. There never seems to be any hurry to leave and close the garden. In fact, the facility lists no hours of operation. This is very different from the adjacent kiosks that open their shutters between the hours of 8am and 4pm, during the week, and are closed on the weekends. In discussions with the workers at the farm, it became clear that several of them live in the high-rise buildings located behind the garden, often with many people living within the same household. Several units within the building lack proper ventilation, making them extremely hot in the summer. The garden and market offer shelter and respite from the heat and the overcrowded dwellings. The garden is fragrant and quite different from the surrounding street smells of garbage, exhaust, and sewage. While people from these buildings can be observed on the adjacent street corners, socialising while sitting under the shade of the trees or playing soccer, the activity in the garden is different—perhaps as it is more purposeful and there is an opportunity to make money while there. Relatives seem to frequently visit the site to convey messages, pick up some items for dinner, or to just sit in the shade for a while. Social interactions with people passing in the street are also evident at this garden and the surrounding kiosks. People stop to chat, shake hands, or even just acknowledge each other. Rarely does someone pass by without offering a greeting.

While the shopping experience involves social interaction, it is also about necessity, negotiation, cunning, timing, and survival. The early morning and late afternoon are the busiest within this neighbourhood, and women seem to assume the main responsibility for this within households. Armed with bags and handmade trolleys, they look as if they are taking part in a strategic manoeuvre more than a shopping expedition. Most perishable food is grown locally and is only seasonally available. The scarcity at each market initiates heated discussions among customers about availability elsewhere in the community and this often leads to a frenzy of activity. Assessing the limited options, but not wanting to purchase inferior products, these consumers must determine whether it is worth walking to a different store to make that perfect acquisition for dinner or lunch. So, while there is conviviality surrounding shopping at the garden, there is also a determination to find the required item before one's neighbour purchases it from an alternative location. This garden—due to its locally grown greens and connections in Guanabacoa—has different produce than that found in the surrounding markets, making it an important stop for provisioning.

Garbage also adds an important rhythm to the streets surrounding the garden (Figure 5.6). There are multiple dumping locations around the site. The exact position of these dumpsters is subject to constant subtle change, as the line of bins and the adjacent heap of refuse migrates back and forth along the street. On one side, dumpsters only partially contain the garbage, while on the other side of the garden it is strewn in a pile at the side of the road. While the municipality should be picking up the garbage every day, this rarely occurs. Several people informed me that the workers often steal fuel from the garbage trucks, to make extra money. As they do not want to draw attention to the missing diesel, they periodically overlook pick-ups within certain neighbourhoods.

Figure 5.6 shows the locations of garbage throughout the neighbourhood at one moment in time. Bins are always located next to sites of collapse or gardens as no one wants to live adjacent to the mess or smell, especially as these locations also serve as the neighbourhood public toilet with people using the bins for privacy. According to CUJAE professors and students, each container is meant to serve approximately 490 people for one day. Households drop off garbage on the way to work or school, often several times a day, to keep the odours out of their homes. Sometimes this job is designated to the children or elderly members of a household. People pick through the garbage: some look for bottles or metals, some for useful abandoned household items. The glass and plastic bottles are often collected by the workers in the garden for use as containers or to create an edging for a raised planting bed. Tins are a valuable commodity. Here, the collectors flatten the tins and recycle the aluminium. The rhythmic beating of metal in Cayo Hueso can be heard through the streets of the neighbourhood surrounding this garden.

With only a metal gate separating most dwellings from the street, domestic life in Cayo Hueso is on display. One can observe, hear, and smell many activities, including the aromas of mealtimes, families watching soap operas, religious practices, and the noise of ongoing home renovations. One resident on the street across from the garden is enlarging the cistern under

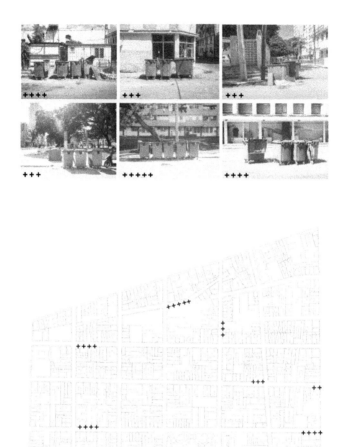

Figure 5.6 Karen Mills: number and location of garbage bins, 2018

Graphics by Stavros Kondeas, Rita Wang, Alicia McDowell (Gilmore), and Lucas McDowell

his home so the household can endure the intermittent water supply. As the dirt extracted from digging this cistern was wheeled out daily to form part of the growing heap of garbage, it was collected by the gardeners to fill their cultivation beds. Such was the need for the soil, the workers helped by ferrying the soil across the road.

Sounds change from day to night. The sounds of traffic and honking horns are replaced by quieter music and hushed conversations as the sun sets. Afternoon drumming takes place within the courtyards of the multi-unit residences to call the Santería saints, while bici-taxi drivers blare their own jarring personal soundtracks, oblivious to others as they cycle along the streets looking for fares. Around the garden, a tiny pocket of more natural sounds can be heard that includes birds during the day; their chirping being replaced by the sounds of crickets at night.

Other creatures are also part of the streetscape. Outside the butcher's kiosk, cats wait patiently for scraps in the early morning and again at closing time. Dogs run freely through the market. No one takes much notice of their activities. The infirm and the elderly are also part of these streets. One elderly lady, dressed in what appears to be her nightdress, wanders into the garden several times a day. Her neck brace suggests she has recently had a fall. While she seems confused in her movements, she clutches a mango as she emerges from the market area. In the Western world, one rarely sees the elderly in the streets or the market, especially those suffering from dementia, as they have been removed from everyday life. One of the workers gently directs the woman to the right and she continues on her way. I saw her most days in the streets surrounding the market and sometimes at the adjacent Sistema de Atención a la Familia, a facility in the community that offers free meals and provisions to supplement the diets of the lower-income, often elderly, population. She wandered around her neighbourhood, with the trace of a smile, in her own little world.

New Airbnbs or *casa particulares* are sprouting up in this community; clearly visible as patches of new paint on the otherwise dilapidated façades, where random floors of buildings are being renovated. Along with the cosmetic overhaul, these buildings are secured and internalised. Airbnb has changed the way tourists engage with the city. They typically stay longer, spend more time in local neighbourhoods, and cause the rhythms in the neighbourhoods to oscillate. Tourists want refuge and, while they are typically happy to be part of this community, they require enhanced safety and privacy. Such spaces are different to the everyday transparent and permeable life of Cayo Hueso.

From all of this, the most evident rhythm of all in this neighbourhood is the prevalence of what Karen Dubinsky calls 'sociolismo' versus 'socialismo'—this involves reciprocity among *socios* and neighbours as opposed to the 'state ideology (socialism)'.[22] Sometimes this practice involves neighbours helping the elderly, the santeros or santeras sourcing medicinal plants for believers, or the network of gossip that facilitates daily provisioning, all within a neighbourhood where everybody is known and acknowledged. These practices are embedded in the everyday life of this community and are evident in its rhythms.

5.4 Documenting Everyday Life

The Green Map is a global movement that involves localities documenting 'social, economic, and ecological assets in a community' through mapping and local knowledge. Wendy Brawer implemented this concept in Centro Habana so people living in the area could more fully understand their neighbourhood. Such a process leads to a recognition of attributes and local solutions to challenges.[23] The neighbourhood is evaluated by using established graphic icons (from the Green Map) and encouraging the community to create site-specific ones. While these maps reflect positive attributes of the neighbourhood (such as parks, gyms, or schools), they include things or programmes rather than the complex social interactions that take place over time. Using a similar mapping technique but one that also documents networks and rhythms is geared towards a greater understanding of how the citizens of this community successfully live together, over time, within these partially collapsed buildings, in often very crowded circumstances.

The strong social connections are particularly salient in the face of crisis. In 2017, Hurricane Irma caused damage to 12 of Cuba's 15 provinces and forced approximately two million people to leave their homes. Shelters in Cayo Hueso were not formalised, but involved displaced people staying with family and friends, on higher ground, a few blocks away from the flood zone. The storm surge burst through the walls along the Malecón and water flooded six blocks beyond the seawall. Similarly, there was the Storm of the Century in 1993 and, in 2005, Hurricane Wilma.[24] While these cataclysmic events occur approximately every 12 years, many other annual events flood low-lying areas, continually jeopardising the dilapidated housing stock. While the garden in Cayo Hueso is above the flood zone, the salt-laden wind that accompanied Hurricane Irma burnt the plants. Not only did neighbours accommodate friends and relatives but they also helped with the communal clean-up of the streets and the garden. While these activities do not precisely locate the boundaries of a frame or 'pocket world', this sense of a caring community with resilience seems to be inextricably linked to all aspects of living and working in Cayo Hueso.

Finding the pocket world surrounding the garden involved locating the symbiotic everyday programmes. These include those provided by the state, including free education and healthcare, and the stores that stock subsidised food. It meant documenting the nearby schools and nurseries that attend classes at the garden (Figure 5.8). Other organizations have less formal relationships with the garden. Medical *consultorios* regularly send patients to purchase remedies, and green pharmacies stock products acquired from the site (Figure 5.9). Likewise, cafeterias for low-income residents, the so-called Sistema de Atención a la Familia (SAF), produce food from the vegetables grown in the garden and provide a place to sit and eat near by. Herbs are harvested and delivered to the local care home for the elderly and to the house for pregnant women that are located at the periphery of the community. In this Afro-Cuban neighbourhood, Santería is practiced in many (if not most) of the homes. Santero(a)s frequent the garden to pick plants from the beds that, since they are picked directly from the earth, have heightened potency. Parque de Trillo, two blocks away, is a site of religious significance with offerings from the garden left at the base of the four large ceiba trees that mark the corners of the park. All of these activities form an interconnected game-board surrounding the garden.

Ultimately, there is a protagonist in this community who rallies many of these networks. This person is part social activist, entrepreneur, and bricoleur. He connects people, places, and processes to make things happen. In Cayo Hueso, this has involved creating a garden and market for trading that is not exclusively about buying and selling but provides a space where people can socialise and rest out of the sun. Such a typology does not typically exist; it is a hybrid space—somewhere in-between a community centre, a doctor's waiting room, and a garden all integrated into one. This site differs from the one located in San Isidro as anyone can enter the space where things grow. It is not reserved for workers and school children but is a place for all. In such a dilapidated community, having a space of growth and fragrance, where one can wander among planted beds, is an important asset and as significant as it is for food production. It is also part of a broader network of places to shop for food, some formal and others informal. The map showing provisioning activity includes the garden and its surrounding kiosks, markets, cafeterias, *bodegas*, and multiple mobile street carts (Figure 5.7). These outlets connect people to spaces where they can grow, sell, and buy food within the neighbourhood.

The Consultorios Tiendas Agropecuarios (CTA) is adjacent to the garden. The word *consultorio* is used in a similar way to a local doctor's office (also called a *consultorio*), emphasising the informative nature of the resource over the commercial value.[25] CTAs advise the community on urban farming and gardening in general. They offer technical and advisory services to clients who are already engaged in agriculture, and they hold beginner workshops for those with an interest in growing food. Each CTA supplies seeds, ornamental and medicinal plants, and fruit trees. In addition, they stock gardening tools for rent, and government-approved fertilisers and pesticides. The CTA in Cayo Hueso stocks multiple varieties of seeds, including garlic, cauliflower, spinach, tomato, pepper, Swiss chard, broccoli, eggplant, pumpkin, red radish, turnip, and beet. They also sell pots and books and distribute brochures on specific topics. According to the workers, there are 175 similar outlets throughout Cuba that share information and give advice to citizens on gardening. This central repository of information links urban agricultural knowledge across the country.[26] A community space that has benefited from the CTA's educational service is at the centre of the adjacent block; residents have appropriated the area for gardening and planted banana trees and vegetables. What was once a space where garbage collected has become a productive urban farm. The residents consume the garden's harvest, and the excess produce is sold in the adjacent market. This space is also used for relaxation and recreation as it shades the surrounding apartments from the sun. A gate was installed making this space only accessible to the residents of the block. Cultivation has encouraged the residents to make insurgent claims on the space that has both improved their diets and their living environment.

5.4.1 Drift

Figures 5.7, 5.8, and 5.9 document the programmes and activities that relate to provisioning, education, and healthcare. These maps shed light on many details about daily life and its nuanced rhythms. Based upon observation and informal interviews, they trace the typical routes citizens use to obtain provisions, attend school, and procure healthcare in Cayo Hueso. Obtaining food is controlled by the government and the stores where citizens obtain the subsidised items listed in the Libreta de Abastecimiento (supplies booklet) are proximal to where people live. These shops supply dried goods, typically rice, sugar, and beans, at very low prices. Meat is bought at the local *carnicería* and milk at the *lechería*. Both store types are typically located on street corners. They were sometimes hard to recognise, with no advertising and so few items within the store, it took many passes through the community to identify all these types of stores. The designated products were often not available and randomly arrived throughout the day, resulting in the shop either being closed or having long queues when stock finally arrived. Luxury items, such as tinned goods, were purchased from the CUC store and the stock was very dependent on the ever-evolving supply chains. One week, there were tins of tuna, while the next, it was kippers. For fresh fruit and vegetables, there was more choice within close proximity. Some of the prices were government controlled while others were not. The businesses that regulated their prices often had lower quality products. All of the markets carried seasonal fruits and vegetables that would not spoil in transit when brought in from farms outside the city. Leafy greens were generally only available in this area, fresh from Organopónico de Alto Rendimiento. The drift map revealed the time-consuming nature and uncertainty of provisioning. However, what was also apparent was that shopping in this neighbourhood was a highly social activity that involved frequent stops to gossip in addition to buying. Both activities—talking and provisioning—appeared to be equally important within a community where people know each other and the street works as a social public space. Mobile markets are also part of the street life. These can be found stationary at street corners or as carts that move around, with the proprietor selling the produce by walking the street and yelling out their wares for sale. Customers hoist the food up on a pulley system, so people with limited mobility or time do not need to leave their homes to provision.

Gardening and growing are activities that are important to the community, and they want to get accurate information. People who stopped at the CTA spent a great deal of time discussing their plant concerns with the staff. While they rarely appeared to purchase anything, they did seek detailed advice and often showed up with a potted plant, clippings, or seeds to discuss. Also, they often left with the free leaflets outlining specific information to address their concerns. Clients often stayed at the CTA for over 30 minutes, and it was not uncommon to see an hour-long consultation. When there were no customers, the CTA staff chatted with the shop assistants at the adjacent kiosks or with the producers at the garden. Conversations with the workers revealed they were all highly knowledgeable about cultivation and many held agricultural degrees and had practical experience in multiple scales of farming.

Figure 5.9 highlights the relationship between the pharmacy across the street and the garden. After having waited in line at the pharmacy for almost an hour, customers often crossed the road to enter Organopónico de Alto Rendimiento. As the pharmacy often did not have the requested medicine in stock, the helpful pharmacist recommended a trip to the green pharmacy (garden) across the street as they did not want to turn people away without suggesting alternatives. The customers often entered the garden clutching a piece of paper to show to the producers, to ensure they were given the correct plant for their ailment. In fact, the garden even grew custom medicinal plants recommended by doctors and pharmacists, although this was weather and time dependent. It was also evident there was much local knowledge on plant medicine. A 15-minute segment on Cuban Radio Rebelde offered remedies every morning. Juan Tomás Roig's popular book *Plantas Medicinales, Aromáticas o Venenosas de Cuba* (Medicinal, aromatic, or poisonous plants of Cuba) is readily available in Cuba.

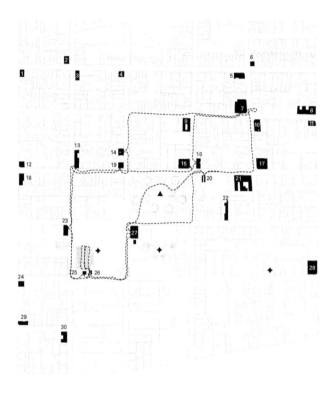

* Productive garden
---- Circulation path
▲ Parque de Trillo

CUC store — 14, 15
Meat and/or eggs — 3, 11, 13, 25
Bakery — 7
Market - bodegas — 1, 2, 4, 5, 6, 8, 9, 10, 12,
16, 17, 18, 19, 21, 22, 23, 24, 25, 28, 29, 30
Market - mercados agropecuarios — 26, 27
Drink Stand — 20

↑ N

Productive Garden   Market, 27   Bodega, 10

Figure 5.7 Drift showing provisioning activity

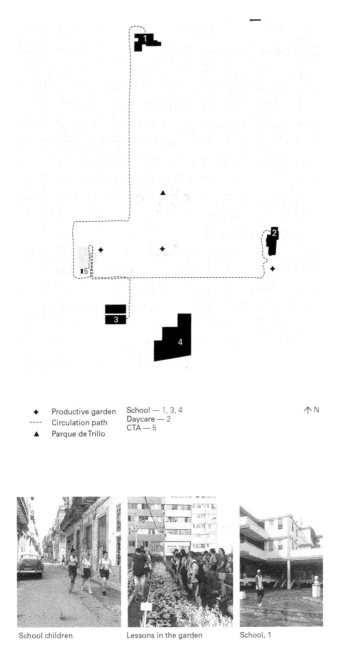

Figure *5.8* Drift of school children and their interaction with the garden

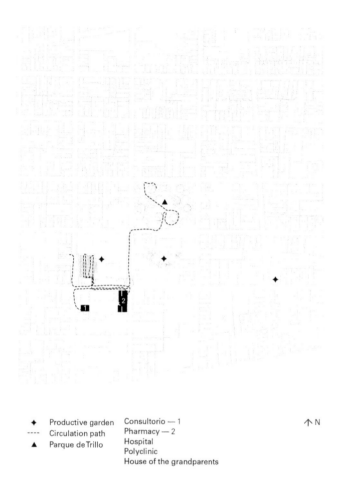

✦	Productive garden	Consultorio — 1	↑ N
----	Circulation path	Pharmacy — 2	
▲	Parque de Trillo	Hospital	
		Polyclinic	
		House of the grandparents	

Green pharmacy   Pharmacy, 2

Figure 5.9 Drift of persons seeking medical treatment

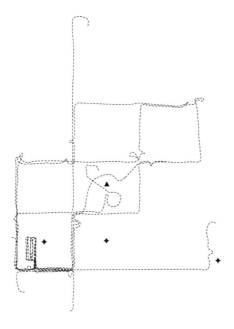

◆ Productive garden
---- Circulation path
▲ Parque de Trillo

↑ N

Space to relax or wait for service in the garden

Figure 5.10 Combined drift activities

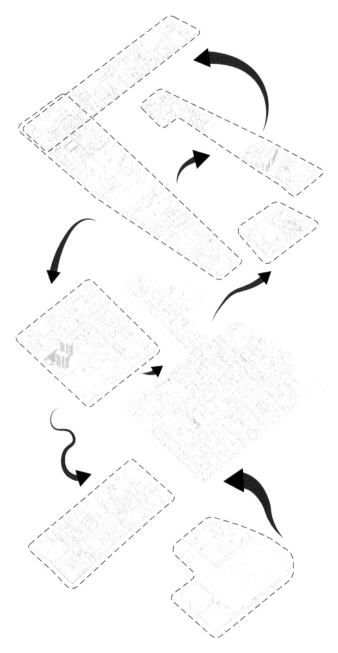

Figure 5.11 Drift in Cayo Hueso showing psychogeographical shifts

Wellbeing, provisioning, healthcare, spirituality, and education all collide surrounding the garden and these drift maps reveal these everyday activities (see Figure 5.10). The shifts in psychogeographical contours within the neighbourhood are shown in Figure 5.11. This drawing demonstrates the changes in perception and rhythms that occur at the main roads where traffic and wider streets hamper access into or out of the community. These include the streets Zanja, Infanta, San Lazaro, and Padre Varela which bracket the neighbourhood. Most of the daily neighbourhood activities occur inside of these roads. Shifts in awareness and everyday life also occur at the only other green space, Parque de Trillo. In this area, the vegetation and shade moderate the temperature and, along with the Wi-Fi access, make it into the social hub of the neighbourhood. By contrast, areas of homogeneous development cause disjuncture, such as industrial zones with large-scale buildings. This occurs within the vicinity of the immense Hospital Hermanos Ameijeiras complex.

These drift and psychogeographical studies locate the patterns and networks of everyday life and demonstrate that they involve social, cultural, and commercial exchanges. The garden, the CTA booth, the juice bar, and the adjacent market are all places where business, conversation, and friendship occur alongside one another. People paused within the market to enjoy the shade of the space and chat with the producers. They did not appear hurried or pressured to buy something and sometimes they left with no produce. Often the customers seemed to be friends or family and their visits were purely social. Once in the garden, they took their time to walk through the beds to select their produce. Sometimes they meandered through several times. Often, they did not purchase anything. It seemed that they enjoyed being among the vegetation, smelling the fragrances, and touching the plants. This contrasted with the actual vegetable market around the corner, where people spent significantly less time lingering and rarely engaged in conversations; this other market focuses on commercial exchange and people go there solely to buy. Provisioning in Cayo Hueso was most active during the early morning and the early evening, as people were coming and going from work, and the garden and streets provided more shade at that time, which made it more pleasant, especially in the summer months.

When all these activities and drawings were superimposed on to one another, it became clear that the garden and the adjacent activities formed a hub in the community. This was not uniquely an economic centre but also an area for social interaction involving conviviality, learning, and culture.

5.4.2 *Layering*

Decay is an important and ever-evolving layer of the city—especially in Cayo Hueso. The extent of the buildings' deterioration was recorded on a map by walking through the streets and in and out of semi-private courtyard spaces. Four levels of decay were recorded: fully collapsed, extensive decay (illegal dwelling only), poor condition, and normal state of construction. Unless there was obvious evidence of illegal dwelling, the inhabitants of Cayo Hueso did not treat the inspections of their properties with suspicion. These assessments were visual only and conducted predominantly from outside of peoples' homes. They were performed both individually and accompanied by students. Often, as a group, we were invited into peoples' homes as Cuban citizens are used to having their living conditions, like their health, scrutinised and want to discuss it with you so you fully understand the extent of the damage to their homes, especially if they believe that you might have an impact on the neighbourhood's repair schedule or have access to materials. However, those families living within dwellings in a state of imminent collapse were more anxious and repeatedly stressed how pleased they were with the present condition of their homes, as if trying to postpone their inevitable eviction even if their circumstances were clearly extremely dangerous. As outlined before, Cuban citizens only own their dwelling unit. The Cuban state owns the land on which these dwelling units are situated. When a building collapses, the land the building occupied reverts back to the state. For Cubans, this fear is associated with the knowledge that they could soon be relocated and lose their main asset—their home. As there are no resources to rebuild the dwellings once the detritus has been removed, these sites often remain vacant for decades, while the families move into so-called refugee shelters in different neighbourhoods, far from their local networks and rhythms.

The damage and decay are extensive in Cayo Hueso. At the current rate of decay, time will only make the destruction of the city worse. The maps in Figure 5.12 shows how many buildings are expected to fall if the decay is not abated. This drawing suggests that any response needs to be as much about shoring up and securing as about building new structures. This is important as the collapse of one building damages many of the surrounding properties, which leads to an even larger problem. As collapses typically occur from the top down, the lower units below must be secured from falling debris and weather, as they often no longer have a roof and they must be protected from the elements.

There are benefits that have emerged out of this decay that are cyclical in nature. It is impossible to plan for precise materials to construct things at sites of urban agriculture. The only guaranteed products are household refuge and the debris that can be acquired from a building collapse, but it is never known exactly what will be available at the time of construction. Using scavenged rubble as part of a cyclical process of collapse and growth is a strange way to repair or build the structures in the garden. This temporal activity

Current state of collapsing buildings

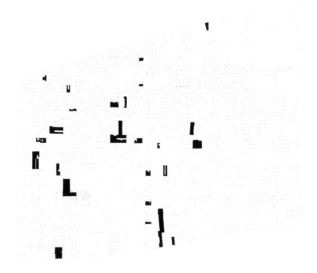

Predicted future collapses if construction issues are not alleviated

Figure 5.12 Layering collapse of buildings over time in Cayo Hueso

has winners and losers, as opportunists (so-called rubble-lists) recover the decaying materials and others use them for construction projects.

> Firstly, [there is] the sand product of the collapse that is used in a mix with cement, and [this is] certainly very popular in new constructions. Secondly, the old, whole bricks are highly valued for building walls. Thirdly, the beams that once endured supporting the structures are preserved given the quality of the wood, and then are used in construction. Some lose, and others win; respectively, the poor seniors that live here and from now on until their death in a shelter, and these opportunists (called by Cubans *escombreadores*) who later sell a sack of sand for 50 pesos.[27]

Such is the situation that old materials are used to build the new parts of the city. This is an incremental approach where things are built from what has collapsed. Depending upon what has crumbled, bricks, tiles, and concrete in multiple shapes and textures can be used. These materials are placed by people whose skills have developed, over many years, to become adept at making do, in piecing together the irregular, the broken, and the different. It is a palimpsestic process, a way of making the decay useful. The new constructed artifacts have a memory of what once was. A particular part of a wall is recognised as part of this new city and is simultaneously its past layer and its future one.

Since 2010, the Cuban National Housing Institute has permitted the selling of building materials to the public. Prior to this, only the government had access to construction resources. Despite efforts, the system remains rampant with corruption, as Cubans with *socios* within the institute can purchase these materials and then resell them to the public at higher rates. This means that large sectors of the population have very little access to building materials, while others are making money from it. For example, from September 2017 to September 2018, the cost of a bag of state supplied concrete rose from 6 to 15 CUCs. The crumbling buildings and sparse shipments determine the presence of materials in the marketplace. So people are exploring experimental products: walls made from gabion baskets filled with rubble from collapsed buildings; structural members, such as columns and roof trusses, constructed from rebar; bamboo structures made from the fast-growing grass that flourishes in the climate; and planters constructed from bottles, roof tiles, and pipe.

5.4.3 Game-Board

The game-board reading of the place involved uncovering the symbiotic relationships in the community—teasing out the reciprocal relationships that people and things have within this vegetated space in the city. These connections enabled multiple opportunities to unfold and have been documented throughout the narrative and drawings in this chapter. The activities surrounding the garden evolved throughout the day, week, and over the years. They include

- The constant comings and goings within the community to the market and garden—a place that provides both a source of income for the producers while supplementing the community's access to food and medicine.
- Children regularly attend classes and circles of interest at the garden and so knowledge, teaching, and education are exchanged within the community.
- Medical *consultorios* and pharmacies sent patients to the garden to purchase green medicine from the site. This helps to alleviate the scarcity of allopathic medications and creates revenue for the garden.
- The garden provides free herbs and vegetables for the Sistema de Atención a la Familia (SAF). Herbs and leafy greens are also delivered to the elderly in the community and to a local house for pregnant women. This creates good will in the community and this, in turn, helps secure the garden's ongoing usufruct use of the land.
- The garden provides a green space that is accessible to the community and serves as a market, a garden, a community centre, and a pharmacy. To enter and enjoy requires no financial outlay.
- Santero(a)s frequent the garden to pick plants from the beds. Producers learn from their informed customers about the plants they need for their Santería rituals, and this in turn, helps preserve the culture within the community.
- During afternoon downpours, water is collected from the roofs of the adjacent buildings and used to fill the garden's water tank. This helps alleviate the flooding in the streets while contributing irrigation water to the plants.
- Conviviality is very apparent amongst customers, passers by, neighbours, assistants, and producers.
- Other businesses have collected around this garden, thereby creating a localised hub for commerce.

5.4.4 Rhizome

The existing typological and morphological rhythms of buildings within this neighbourhood are important to study. *Cuarterías* and *ciudadelas* are the most prevalent forms of housing for a population that fluidly intermixes living, working, growing, and playing, often with all three occupying the same space and spilling out onto the street. While reviewing the present and future collapse in the city (as documented in Figure 5.12), a surprising rhizomic relationship started to emerge; there is a direct relationship between the quality of living spaces and the size and number of the courtyards. Figure 5.2 shows how ventilation spaces are incorporated into dwellings within the city. Due to the intense heat, high humidity, and very tight living situations, maintaining ventilation is one of the most important strategies for comfort and healthy living. People flourish in dwellings that maintain their ventilation spaces and do not permit subversive development. Growing plants in these courtyard spaces improves the air quality and reduces the climatic temperature, thereby easing tension in these dense environments. People do not block access routes to their homes and so combining the semi-public space with horizontal and vertical circulation maintains the voids and prevents insurgent development.

5.5 Conclusion

So great is the density in Cayo Hueso that people often sleep in shifts due to overcrowding and housing shortages. Many families live in a single room, with minimal cooking and shared bathing and laundry facilities. Like many facets of Cuban culture, one space fulfils many purposes, including living, working, and growing. Institutions such as the Sistema de Atención a la Familia and local cafeterias provide a place where people can obtain cheap meals and sit for a while. Likewise, the garden creates a space for both being connected or alone in such density. Roland Barthes reflected on this and offered 'the concept of "idiorrhythmy"' that recognised the need for multiple rhythms to be respected within communities. Such a place 'allows for approximation, for imperfection'.[28] Barthes provided multiple examples from literature to discuss how socio-spatial struggles are reconciled through 'idiorrhythmy'. This garden in Cayo Hueso is emblematic of this and is very permissive of and adaptive to the multiple rhythms within the community. It operates as a game-board with many symbiotic relationships coming together in a similar way to John F.C. Turner's Open Services Network (versus what he referred to as the Closed Project Hierarchy) in his book *Freedom to Build*. Turner used this model to demonstrate different ways of constructing housing in Lima, Peru. The Open Services Network helped people leverage the broad range of services that could be found in their networks of *socios*, family members, and friends. It presented 624 combinations versus the closed project where options were quite limited. In Cayo Hueso, the provisioning of food and medicine, although in small supply, operates as an open services network. The use of resource networking is visible everywhere in Cayo Hueso. Spaces such as Organopónico de Alto Rendimiento are integral to filling in the gaps and facilitating everyday life in Cuba.[29]

Notes

1. Felicia Chateloin, "Una Mirada a La Historia Urbana De Centro Habana: La Necesidad Del Reconocimiento," in *Centro Habana: Un Futuro Sustentable*, ed. Gina Rey (La Habana: Facultad de Arquitectura de La Universidad de La Habana, 2009), 28.
2. Guadalupe García, *Beyond the Walled City: Colonial Exclusion in Havana* (Oakland: University of California Press, 2016), 25.
3. Ariadna D. Fernandez and Leonora Angeles, "Building Better Communities: Gender and Urban Regeneration in Cayo Hueso, Havana, Cuba," *Women's Studies International Forum* 32, no. 2 (2009): 80.
4. Anguelovski, *Neighborhood as Refuge Community Reconstruction, Place Remaking, and Environmental Justice in the City*, 82.
5. Chateloin, "Una Mirada a La Historia Urbana De Centro Habana: La Necesidad Del Reconocimiento," 29.
6. City Population, "City Population".
7. Fernandez and Angeles, "Building Better Communities: Gender and Urban Regeneration in Cayo Hueso, Havana, Cuba," 81.
8. Chateloin, "Una Mirada a La Historia Urbana De Centro Habana: La Necesidad Del Reconocimiento," 33.
9. Jerry Spiegel et al., "Building Capacity in Central Havana to Sustainably Manage Environmental Health Risk in an Urban Ecosystem," *EcoHealth; Conservation Medicine: Human Health: Ecosystem Sustainability* 1, no. 2 (2004): 121.
10. Fernandez and Angeles, "Building Better Communities: Gender and Urban Regeneration in Cayo Hueso, Havana, Cuba," 81.
11. Mark Kurlansky, *Havana: A Subtropical Delirium* (London: Bloomsbury, 2017), 179.
12. Scarpaci, Segre and Coyula, *Havana: Two Faces of the Antillean Metropolis*, 162.
13. Coyula, *Understanding Slums: The Case of Havana, Cuba*, 28.
14. Coyula, *Understanding Slums: The Case of Havana, Cuba*, 28
15. United Nations Human Settlements Programme, *The Challenge of Slums Global Report on Human Settlements, 2003* (London: Earthscan Publications, 2003), 11.
16. Holston, *Insurgent Citizenship: Disjunctions of Democracy and Modernity in Brazil*, 8–9.
17. Claude Lévi-Strauss, *The Savage Mind* (Chicago: University of Chicago Press, 1966), 17.
18. Ministerio de Salud Pública, *Ministerio de Salud Pública Resolución Ministerial No. 381*, (La Habana: La República de Cuba Ministerio de Justicia, 2015).
19. Gold, *People and State in Socialist Cuba: Ideas and Practices of Revolution*, 50.
20. George Brandon, "The Uses of Plants in Healing in an Afro-Cuban Religion, Santería," *Journal of Black Studies* 22, no. 1 (1991): 58.
21. Brandon, "The Uses of Plants in Healing in an Afro-Cuban Religion, Santería," 60.
22. Karen Dubinsky, *Cuba beyond the Beach: Stories of Life in Havana* (Toronto: Between the Lines, 2016), 7.

23. Maeve Lydon, ed., *Mapping Our Common Ground a Community and Green Mapping Resource Guide* (Victoria: Common Ground, 2007), 13.
24. Tanya Zakrison. "The Medical, Public Health, and Emergency Response to the Impact of 2017 Hurricane Irma in Cuba," *Disaster Medicine and Public Health Preparedness* 14, no. 1 (2020): 10–17.
25. Luc J. A. Mougeot, *Agropolis: The Social, Political and Environmental Dimensions of Urban Agriculture* (Ottawa: International Development Research Centre, 2005), 180.
26. INIFAT, "Los Consultorios-Tiendas Del Agricultor, Una Opción Cada Vez Más Viable Para Los Productores," www.ausc.co.cu/index.php/72-los-consultorios-tiendas-del-agricultor-una-opcion-cada-vez-mas-viable-para-los-productores (accessed December 2018).
27. Mario Hechevarria-Driggs, "A New Collapse in Havana," *Cubalog.Eu*, http://cubalog.eu/2016/02/a-new-collapse-in-havana/ (accessed 23 June 2018).
28. Roland Barthes, *How to Live Together: Novelistic Simulations of Some Everyday Spaces* (New York: Columbia University Press, 2013), back cover and 35.
29. Brotherton, *Revolutionary Medicine: Health and the Body in Post-Soviet Cuba*, 168.

6 The Complex Character of Plaza de la Revolución

6.1 Background

Plaza de la Revolución is the name of both a municipality and Havana's largest public plaza. As a municipality, it encompasses the districts (*Consejos Populares*) of Vedado and Nuevo Vedado. The municipality's population is approximately 140,000, and its density is 11,500 inhabitants per square kilometre, making it significantly less occupied than Centro Habana or La Habana Vieja.[1] As a square, the plaza celebrates one of Cuba's most important revolutionaries, José Martí, while it also portrays the evolving power of the state. As a municipality, it is simultaneously urban and rural. Both large-scale political mobilisations and small-scale manifestations of the Revolution are encountered within this part of the city, making it an interesting site for studying urban rhythms.

The plaza was originally built as a space for parking vehicles; but after the triumph of the Revolution, it was reimagined as a place for the state to communicate the evolving ideas of the new Cuba, a place where the government meets the people through large-scale state-sponsored political and cultural events. Over one million people participate in the annual International Workers' Day, held on the first day of May every year. There are also the occasional July 26 celebrations, marking the Moncada Barracks attack at the start of the Revolution. After Fidel Castro's death, the square hosted a two-day commemoration for their beloved leader. Peace without Borders II, a large music concert, occurred in 2009, and hundreds of thousands of Cubans attended Masses Pope John Paul II and Pope Francis celebrated in the square in 1998 and 2015, respectively. Bordered on three sides by major arterial roads, the José Martí Memorial dominates this vast concrete and asphalt expanse (Figure 6.1). Its five-sided star-shaped tower and the massive marble sculpture of José Martí are located at one of the highest points in the city. The seat of government—the Palace of Justice—wraps around part of the José Martí monument, while the space within the memorial is dedicated to

DOI: 10.4324/9781003201410-6

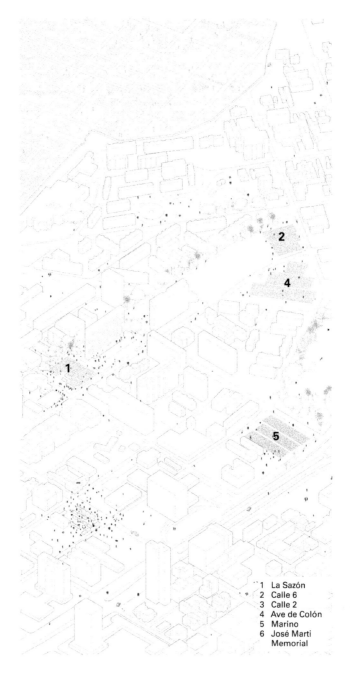

1 La Sazón
2 Calle 6
3 Calle 2
4 Ave de Colón
5 Marino
6 José Martí
   Memorial

Figure 6.1 Axonometric drawing of the Plaza de la Revolución neighbourhood

Figure 6.1 (Continued)

correspondence, drawings, writings, and other items that commemorate the life of this revolutionary martyr. This square was originally constructed as Plaza Cívica, during Fulgencio Batista's dictatorship, and it was completed in 1955.[2] In 1960, after the Revolution, the state appropriated the square as its own.[3] The area of the square is approximately eleven acres.[4] Containing the large gatherings that often assemble here requires expanding into the land surrounding government buildings. Such massive displays of unity and citizen participation mark the legitimacy of the Revolution and re-orientate the square's purpose into a place of patriotism and solidarity. In fact, the story of Plaza de la Revolución has been re-written several times throughout its history, without there being any structural transformations made to the square but rather through its changing rhythms and patterns. With its surrounding multiple-lane highways, the space was originally conceived of as a central traffic hub, where engagement occurred while driving past at high speed. After the Revolution, the square became a space of choreographed events between the people and the state, as different groups of workers parade past the José Martí monument and the president. With places of work and school closed for the day, participation is strongly encouraged.[5] The Central Organisation of Cuban Trade Unions and the Committees for the Defence of the Revolution are particularly active in encouraging widespread involvement.

After 1990, and the collapse of the Soviet Union, cultural heritage and the collective memory was repositioned surrounding the plaza. In 1993, the seasonally changing image of Che Guevara was immortalised in steel, with Alberto Korda's monumental Guerrillero Heroico (Heroic Warrior), along with with the words 'Hasta la Victoria Siempre' (Until Victory Always) being permanently attached to the five-storey Ministry of Interior. In 2009, an image of the face of Camilo Cienfuego another martyred revolutionary, joined that of Che on the Ministry of Communications, with the words 'Vas bien, Fidel' (You're doing fine, Fidel). Likewise, a museum in the basement of the monument opened to commemorate the life, writing, and work of José Martí. Positioning all of these historic moments within the square distanced Cuba from its connection to the collapsed Soviet Union and indicated an important ideological shift for the country. Fidel Castro, as the 'political philosopher'[6] narrated this transition with speeches from the square, while at the museum the connection between Martí and Castro was curated through an exhibition.[7] Linking the Revolution to Martí and engaging the square and the state with his ethics positioned him and Castro as having shared similar ideologies. The Cuban newspaper, *Granma* published an article entitled 'Two men, the Same Dream' describing how closely aligned these two men were surrounding the themes of patriotism, unity, solidarity, and anti-imperialism.[8] After the 1992 Rio Summit, Fidel Castro considered the environment as being fundamental to Cuba's socialist agenda and intrinsic to its fight against capitalism. Sustainable development was closely linked to what José Martí stood for and 'the very origins of the Revolution—the wars of independence'.[9] With this layering, nature and ecology were positioned as moral objectives alongside the Revolution.

With the change in leadership, in 2008, and the evolving attitudes towards work under Raúl Castro's more pragmatic economic direction, the idea of ecology took on the idea of efficiency and sustainability in work. As the rallies in the square decreased in size, along with Raúl Castro's more limited oratory skills in comparison to his brother's, importance became increasingly placed on financial self-reliance. No longer was it considered the responsibility of the state to secure employment for the population. Along with sustainability, the Revolution encouraged entrepreneurism, through private business. 'In 2013, *cuentapropistas* marched in the Labour Day parade as a group'.[10] So, with almost no structural changes being made to the plaza, as its programmes and the activities around it evolved so did the rhythms of the square and the sub-text of the space.

6.2 The Community

Many places of state employment are located in Plaza de la Revolución, with government ministries, military, and civic buildings located around the plaza, including the Palace of Justice, which houses the offices of the president and the Comité Central of the Partido Comunista de Cuba (PCC); the José Martí National Library; the inter-provincial bus terminal; the Ministry of Communications; the Ministry of the Interior (formally the Office of the Comptroller); the National Theatre; the Ministry of the Revolutionary Armed Forces (former Municipal Palace); the headquarters of the Havana police force; the Ministry of Agriculture; and all of the major state newspapers that operate out of one building.[11] All these make the plaza an important hub within the city. Other rhythms are increasingly important to the community. These include the tourists that frequently visit the plaza as part of the obligatory tour of Havana. They typically arrive mid-morning by taxi, coco-taxi, or double decker London tour bus. Once in the plaza, they venture to the memorial, photograph the José Martí monument, occasionally go to the top of the tower when the elevator is working (it was under repair from 2012 to 2016), and then leave, typically looking confused and sweaty as it is difficult to know exactly where the asphalt square starts and stops. With no shade, the site is brutally hot for much of the year, it also lacks any amenities, and the multiple lanes of traffic have no cross walks or tunnels, which makes it impossible to access the neighbourhoods beyond. Military police control people's movements surrounding the plaza, even insisting on searching their bags. Consequently, beyond the trip to the memorial, few tourists come to this part of the city. So, while this space had been re-appropriated, after the overthrow of the dictator Fulgencio Batista, to represent nationalism and republicanism, it also physically divides the city. While it actively engages citizens through the rallies that take place there, it offers no other facilities or programmes during the rest of the year.

Henri Lefebvre stated that the 'diversion and re-appropriation of space are of great significance, for they teach much about the production of new spaces'.[12] In the *Production of Space*, Lefebvre differentiates 'appropriated space' from the concept of possessed space. Appropriation involves humans transforming a space and this is quite different from a dominated space that has been overpowered. The dichotomy between appropriated and dominated space highlights a peculiar tension in the case of Plaza de la Revolución. The re-appropriation of the square enables society and the state to meet in this space while it simultaneously controls and separates the adjacent communities. As one moves beyond the plaza and into the neighbourhood, a similar yet different re-appropriation is at work as spaces and economies manoeuvre between the state and the citizens in a much more nuanced way.

The neighbourhood surrounding Plaza de la Revolución evolved out of a series of disparate social housing projects, with the interstitial spaces between them poorly considered. Each of the numerous prefabricated buildings in this area had a state sponsor that facilitated the project. These included the Ministries of Transport, the Armed Forces, the Interior, and Labour and Social Security. Initially, people who worked for the specific employer inhabited the buildings their employer constructed. Consequently, many people who live in this part of the city are associated with the government or the military. However, since state reforms have made private initiatives more flexible, homeowners are now renting or selling these apartments to other people and this area is slowly diversifying. In addition, as state employment is so poorly paid, people are pursuing different options or second jobs, alongside their public-sector employment. State employment often supplies access to the internet and other resources—sometimes facilitating these alternative opportunities. These second jobs do not 'represent an opposition to the Revolution, rather they are the vanguard of a revolutionary economy'.[13] These private endeavours, unlike state employment, have developed efficiencies both economically and ecologically. Many of the left-over in-between spaces in this area have become the sites of alternative employment that includes endeavours such as urban farming (Figure 6.2) and food production, mobile flower carts, or juice stands. The re-occupation and re-orientation of these in-between spaces has stitched the community together, surrounding Plaza de la Revolución, in a manner not experienced in its infrequent use during large-scale political rallies. These appropriated spaces—and their associated social activities and networks—embody a type of revolutionary space that is quite different from that of the adjacent plaza. These urban farms and gardens (Figure 6.1) practice ecological and economic sustainability by providing local food and medicine for their communities.

The urban and agrarian reforms of the Revolution were intended to liberate the land that was caught in-between the conflicting values that existed between the countryside and the city centre, and these urban agriculture projects continue with this tradition. In 1968, the Cordón de La Habana plan (green belt), promoted the integral development of the environment surrounding the Cuban capital. It involved the cultivation of approximately 89,000 hectares of agricultural land at the edge of the city. Cultivating close to the population engaged the urban labour force and reduced the distance required to transport the agricultural products to the city. Unfortunately, the implementation of the scheme was flawed as the types of crops grown were inappropriate for the terrain and climate. However, there was, as Kevin Lynch suggested, something more important about this strategy of mixing the country and the city. This tradition continues as these vegetated spaces throughout Plaza de la Revolución permeate through the city, allowing the 'country to reach back into the city'.[14]

The 'communal achievement'[15] of these vegetated spaces has become more profound as the farmers' commitments have evolved. With the collapse of the Soviet Union, the production of green medicine and food became government concerns and a matter of national security. Without necessarily seeing themselves as innovative, the farmers' contributions have made them the Revolution's quiet frontline. The Ministry of Agriculture and the local CDRs have recognised and supported these efforts and through an inspection programme have rewarded sites and outstanding producers for their abundant yields and altruistic community efforts. The designation given to those spaces that have excelled within the urban agriculturalist's profession is *patios* de *referencia* (model patios) and this has elevated the activity from an individual effort to one that has served the community and, consequently, the Revolution.[16]

6.3 The Garden

Some of these farms provide food for the surrounding ministries, while all help feed the community. A conversation with the managers at the La Sazón, the organopónico at the corner of Lombillo and Panorama, confirmed that this farm is part of a larger enterprise with other growing locations nearby. This farm started operating in 2006 on a site that was left over from adjacent housing projects that had been built in the 1980s. The ground was not suitable for development due to the aquifer beneath the site, which made

Figure 6.2 Stavros Kondeas: view of La Sazón, 2019

Graphics by Stavros Kondeas, Rita Wang, Alicia McDowell (Gilmore), and Lucas McDowell

the earth too wet. The state provided the land to the enterprise in usufruct for a renewable period of 20 years. La Sazón now provides food to the local community. In addition, it supplies subsidised food to the local *casa de los abuelos* (house of the grandparents), a daycare programme for the elderly implemented throughout Cuba. Free food is also delivered to pregnant women living in the neighbourhood. Children from two local schools regularly work at the garden so they can learn about urban agriculture. The workers give lectures at the local high school and take part in the *expoferias*. These are expositions that showcase the successes of urban agriculture and disseminate information to a national audience. These educational, social, and healthcare programmes help justify the continued use of the land in the eyes of the community.

Agricultural activities have been part of the curriculum in Cuban schools since 1960. School farming programmes have further gained momentum since the scarcity of the 1990s, a time marked by profound national food shortages. The Ministry of Education requires all Cuban children to have access to gardens and participate in agricultural production. Realised through what is called the labour education stream of courses at schools, these classes develop practical skills, including the preparation of land for cultivation, understanding the calendar for the planting of different crops, creating and using organic fertilisers and pesticides, as well as different sowing methods. While the students' growing spaces within these agricultural locations are meant to be adjacent to their schools, this is invariably impossible due to the lack of resources or land, so schools have typically become affiliated with local urban farms. The interaction between schools and gardens ensures students learn about ethics and ecology as much as about farming.[17] These studies heighten the students' understanding about the nurturing of nature and help them acquire knowledge about different crops and healthy eating habits.[18]

The educational exchanges that take place between these sites of urban agriculture and the schools include lectures at the schools, practical work at the farm, and more informal visits through 'circles of interest'.[19] The labour education class is nationally scheduled for two hours a week and comprises a total of 80 hours of student learning within the school year. Out of that time allocation, according to the producers at La Sazón, during grade five, a student in one of these classes is expected to spend 32 hours studying about urban gardening over the duration of the school year, with 22 hours of work spent within a garden. A similar amount of time is designated for the study and practice of gardening in every grade, from five through nine, making it a significant part of Cuban children's school curriculum. This course involves developing knowledge about the garden, including how these farms contribute to wellness and a more holistic life for the student.

Emphasis is on transforming the mindset of the student from that of a consumer into that of a producer. Along with practical knowledge, the students learn about the life cycles of water, carbon dioxide, and nitrogen, and the preparation of compost, organic humus, and green manures. Sowing and scarification of seeds, hilling and mounding, and irrigation are some of the designated class discussions and techniques students learn. For those interested in future agricultural careers, vocational guidance provides students with information and teaches them about the laws that pertain to the horticulturist working in Cuba. Poultry are part of many urban gardens and are kept by many residents in the city; so the care of chickens, turkeys, and ducks is discussed, including common diseases and parasites. Practical issues are also addressed, such as the construction of feeders and nests for poultry. Such practical knowledge is important where poultry husbandry is a reality in many of the students' daily lives and it is vital to integrate it hygienically into people's homes in the city.[20]

Much about Cuban pedagogy, and particularly any relationship to ecology, is relatable to Cuban children through their studies about José Martí, his life, his ideology, and his writings. Throughout his life, Martí supported the role of nature-based studies in all aspects of formal education. In fact, many schools attempt to have small patches of greenery to mimic a 'jardines martianos' (Martí gardens) and adorn it with statues of Martí and quotes from his poetry. These gardens are promoted to simultaneously evoke patriotic feelings, knowledge of Cuban history, and the protection of the environment. Such spaces have become fragrant sensorial productive places within the schools that combine beauty with hard work. The entire Cuban education programme is centred around these ideas as it attempts to combine 'work, production, and study; emphasising the importance of socially useful subjects' within the curricula.[21] Influenced by José Martí, as well as Friedrich Engels, Karl Marx, and Vladimir Lenin, this process entails the seamless integration of learning and physical work, particularly agriculture, '"Behind every school a field" (287). "In the morning the hoe, in the afternoon [school] work" (285).'[22] This ideology links theory and praxis. The students are also seen to be collectively contributing to the national effort of food security through community engagement. Rather than alienating individuals that perform manual labour, it is mandated alongside their academic work.[23]

The Pioneers is another educational programme attached to agriculture. It includes students from grades one to nine and tries to encourage them to be responsible citizens.[24] It has a profound impact on the everyday life of the school as it encourages academic excellence, organises extracurricular activities, and assists with daily maintenance tasks within the school. Focusing less on the individual and more on the collective, the Pioneers, through elected students, mediate between the authority of the school and the students. The student body has much more responsibility than in Western school systems and students resolve many conflicts themselves before they escalate to involve teachers or the administration. The Pioneers organise interest circles that meet once a week after the school day. These interest circles explore possible future vocations and are instrumental in initiating and engaging students in activities that are associated with various professions and that bridge between the school curriculum and future work. At La Sazón, the workers interact with the different students that come through the various education programmes to help with gardening. These students come to the site most afternoons and assist with daily maintenance tasks that are appropriate to their grade levels.

Seven employees work in the *organopónico* from 7am to 12 noon and from 2pm to 5pm, from Monday to Saturday. The garden is paid a fixed amount for their state quota of vegetables for the *acopio*—this produce is provided at a subsidised rate as it is considered a social contribution to the state. For this farm, the quota of produce has been established at 16 kilograms of vegetables per square metre per year. Above this amount, the farm can sell the produce at market value at their store. One of the labourers explained that once expenses are subtracted, 20% of the profits go to the management of the enterprise, and then any remaining profits are shared amongst the workers—making this a well-paid job in Cuba. The farm grows over 22 crops, including lettuce, basil, chives, oregano, spinach, cucumbers, radishes, carrots, peas, green beans, aloe vera, broccoli, cauliflower, and garlic. Corn is planted in the borders and performs as a natural pesticide. There is a busy point-of-sale market at the edge of the site that includes both a butcher and a produce market. The customers recognise this garden as the best place to purchase meat, fruit, and vegetables in the community. Across the road from the *organopónico* is a bakery and many multi-unit residential housing apartments. The site is currently expanding its production to encompass every available part of the block. They are also constructing another point-of-sale market structure to expand their offerings. La Sazón is affiliated with farms in Mayabeque Province, in the countryside to the east and south of Havana, and the market sells produce from these farms alongside what the local site harvests. While it is generally more expensive than some of the adjacent markets, the variety is greater, and it is always extremely busy.

The site is also affiliated with the local *casa de los abuelos* (house of the grandparents). This local social institution throughout Cuba provides daytime care (for approximately 8–10 hours) to elderly people who cannot care for themselves. These institutions recognise the risk factors that are associated with leaving the elderly alone at home during the day and a variety of physical, recreational, and social activities are organised for the residents.[25] La Sazón partakes in this programme by providing produce for the meals, especially leafy greens, and herbs including oregano, chives, and garlic. The workers make daily deliveries to the care homes and know the residents. The garden also has a few raised garden beds at the facility so the elders can grow herbs and lettuce.

Along with being intimately linked to the timetables of the schools and the homes for the elderly, this place is part of a larger network of food outlets that enable the community to shop within the neighbourhood. Each place specialises in different produce that, in aggregate, enable the local population to provision within a few blocks of their homes. Surrounding the site were two markets, each with a small selection of fruits and vegetables, a busy bakery with large quantities of two types of bread, two highly afford-able cafeterias, and a CUC store for liquor. This farm in Plaza de la Revo-lución plays an important role within the provisioning network and is very much part of the emerging entrepreneurial model for the country.

6.4 Documenting Everyday Life

In 1969, cartographers from the Soviet Union re-drew the National Map of Cuba.[26] Rather than mapping the economic, geographic, or geological land-scape of the country, they captured the country's cultural features within this new national atlas. These maps depicted theatres, museums, and libraries to demonstrate the art and social programmes of the Revolution rather than just its physical or fiscal features. The cultural buildings surrounding the site included the José Martí Library, the José Martí Memorial and museum, and the National Theatre. The National Bus Terminal and the 19th de Noviembre railway station were also included as they linked the community to the rest of the city and country. But one could also include soccer fields and baseball dia-monds to show the mix of social uses. So where does this type of cartography start and stop? Mapping the lived condition of the city involves documenting community assets, including the houses of the grandparents, daycares, the markets, and gardens, and even the linking vegetated parterres. All of these collectively uncover the everyday life of Havana. Embedded within social programmes are spaces for provisioning, education, and healthcare. These networks and their rhythms tell quite a different story than the one attached to the adjacent plaza. These stories are equally important to the Revolution, but their contribution is through everyday praxis.

In a similar manner, two designers—one Cuban and the other French—developed urban strategies to improve everyday life through interactions with nature. Both Jean Claude Nicolás Forestier's master plan developed between 1925 and 1930 and Martinez Inclan's work from several years ear-lier had suggested that the Loma de los Catalanes should be the city's centre;

this is the hill where the José Martí monument and Plaza de la Revolución are now located. The radial and diagonal avenues that now emanate from it were imagined by Forestier as weaving the different neighbourhoods of Havana together through a vegetated and 'scenographic system of parks and parkways' for the enjoyment of the citizens of Havana.[27] In keeping with this cultivated landscape, the Museum of Flora and Fauna and the Ministry of Agriculture were envisioned at the heart of this scheme at the periphery of the plaza. Only the Ministry of Agriculture was actually built, and this is at some distance from the plaza. Forestier's vision developed a strategy for engagement with the landscape.[28] The focus was on a vegetated city, communal and integrated, rather than a type of Haussmannian approach, where the design was about control and dominating the citizens militarily, politically, and socially. While individual pieces of Forestier's master plan were realised, much of the connecting pieces of landscaped tissue were not. However, these productive gardens, vegetated parterres, fallow land, and markets that are interspersed throughout this municipality start to weave together these spaces, linking across the landscape as a vegetated network that is experienced through everyday life. Productive rather than consumptive, this landscape aspires to achieve many of the goals of Forestier's vision.

This part of the city is clearly different from San Isidro and Cayo Hueso. The scale of the streets, the blocks, and the architecture are larger, the population is less dense, and the building stock is generic, newer, and less decayed. Initially, it was harder to find symbiotic relationships and locating a frame around a 'pocket world' seemed less precise. The rhythms that are outlined in Chapter 1 helped to guide this process. *Inventar*, in Plaza de la Revolución, is not so much about survival but entrepreneurialism. *Cuentapropistas* are involved in everyday life throughout this community. Their businesses are not geared towards servicing the tourist industry but rather focus on daily needs. Four busy farmers markets (*mercados agropecuarios*) surround the site. Each offers additional services other than food, such as outlets to buy house plants and flowers, tropical fish, cooking equipment, and watch repair. In aggregate, they allow the population to live well within the community rather than to just survive.

6.4.1 Drift

The drift presents an important device that can be used for understanding that there are breaks or shifts in a community.[29] Surrounding La Sazon, there are multiple places to shop that work in connection with the site, and this enables inhabitants to provision within their neighbourhood. There are also healthcare and therapeutic businesses that utilise the garden's medicinal produce. While the practice of Santería is less evident in Plaza de la

Revolución, there is attention to wellness and green medicine. Two nearby schools regularly attend classes at the garden. However, despite these connections, establishing the exact extent of the game-board was more complicated as the community is less nuanced, and the image of the city is less pronounced. The area's repetitive large-scale residential building blocks made it difficult to understand the specificity of the community until it had been experienced or 'lived' over several weeks, months, and years.

Uncovering areas of exclusion surrounding the site was an important step, particularly in this location. These were areas where access is uncomfortable, difficult, or prohibited—psychogeographical contours that strongly discourage entry into or through certain zones.[30] The six-lane highway of Avenida de la Independencia (also called Avenida de Rancho Boyeros) and the eight lanes of Paseo surrounding the site offer no cross walks, tunnels, or bridges for passage into the community and the nearby Cementerio de Cristóbal Colón is surrounded by a high masonry wall. The fenced railway cut also blocks movement, while the very wide buildings are hard to negotiate around, and guarded political institutions, of which there are many, surround the site. Other psychogeographical contours are more subtle and change throughout the day or year. The intense sun in summer makes it very uncomfortable to walk along certain streets in the neighbourhood from 11am until 4 pm in the afternoon. The extreme length of the blocks exaggerate this as does the lack of shade on certain streets. All these urban readings recognise that the area has barriers.[31] A psychogeographic drawing (Figure 6.3) creates an alternative way of thinking about the city, especially as it can define the boundaries within the community that are quite different from the designations depicted on official maps. Particularly noticeable is the lack of integration between the community and Plaza de la Revolución.

The scale of this neighbourhood is greater than the other two, so the connections between nodes is important. Pedestrian circulation mainly occurs along roads where vegetation grows along the edges of the sidewalks in the parterres. This three-foot band is part of the city street's right-of-way (Figure 6.4). It had been appropriated for food cultivation adjacent to markets and gardens. Along the streets where this strip is planted, the ambient temperature of the sidewalk was cooler, and the air was fragrant as one walked amongst the vegetation. People clearly enjoyed the atmosphere and sometimes stopped to rest on make-shift benches along the way. Children often played in this vegetated zone or stopped to study a plant. Along these streets there was an effort to collect the leaves and clippings. Along the planted routes there was an unofficial organisation of garbage bins being used as organic collection points. The gardens use this plant material in an informal composting strategy that had been implemented surrounding the sites of urban agriculture.

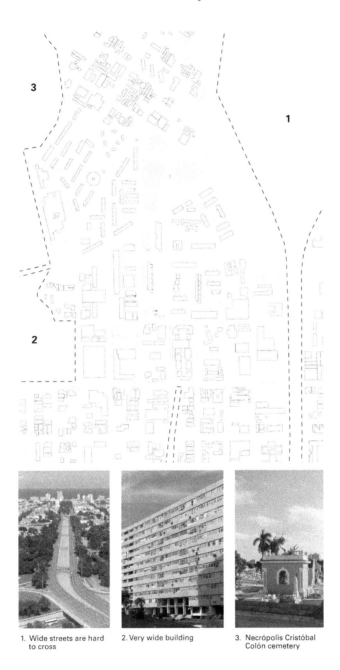

1. Wide streets are hard to cross 2. Very wide building 3. Necrópolis Cristóbal Colón cemetery

Figure 6.3 Psychogeographical contours showing areas of inclusion and exclusion

Figure 6.4 Vegetated parterres

The fallow sites and parterres between the gardens are also used for grazing animals, mainly goats and horses. When the grass is of a sufficient length, the owners tie their animals to stakes so they can graze while their owners return to other activities or take breaks (Figure 6.12 bottom image). This also occurs in-between the buildings and along pathways where these and other local cultivation efforts have made the environment more pleasant and sensorial. State efforts are minimal in keeping the grassy fields cut to facilitate soccer, baseball, or other games. This only occurs on a regular basis around government or tourist facilities, so goats and horses play an important role in keeping fallow land usable for recreation.

Activities surrounding the site were recorded (Figure 6.5–Figure 6.8). Social, cultural, and commercial exchanges were all observed. Conversations and informal meetings were observed as occurring most frequently in the forecourt to the garden market adjacent to the entry to the bakery. People paused outside these spaces to chat with their neighbours. They enjoyed the shade of the surrounding vegetation and the citrus smells. Makeshift benches on rocks were set up and people rested and socialised before or after provisioning. Some entrepreneurs had even opened up their own informal kiosks to take advantage of the crowds of people. But while it was clear that meeting neighbours was important, people went there to buy, and everybody left with purchased goods. There was a greater availability of high-quality perishable leafy greens at this facility than at any of the multiple surrounding markets that tended to stock the same seasonal fruits and vegetables. The bakery was also bustling. The entire space was delightfully fragrant, with the combination of bread baking and fruit smells making it a highly sensorial space. Workers from La Sazón frequently came and went through a small gate into the garden, bringing produce or supplies from the affiliated farms in Mayabeque Province to extend the offerings at the point of sale. La Sazón, including the garden, the forecourt, the market, and surrounding streets, felt energised. This economic and ecological hub, in this community, had quite a different atmosphere from the highly depleted government stores that were situated on the ground floors of the surrounding residential buildings. This is significant in a country with limited entrepreneurial activity and this place has managed to create a certain excitement surrounding shopping.

6.4.2 Game-Board

The game-board involves symbiotic relationships where different people, activities, and things come together and have mutually beneficial interactions. Surrounding this garden these connections can be seen in Figures 6.9 and 6.10 and include the following:

• The garden providing local, fresh food, and green medicine in the community.

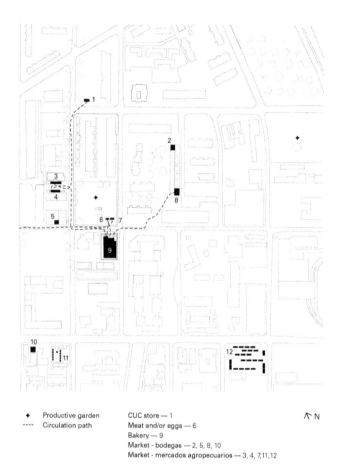

✦   Productive garden   CUC store — 1   ⌐ N
----   Circulation path   Meat and/or eggs — 6
                             Bakery — 9
                             Market - bodegas — 2, 5, 8, 10
                             Market - mercados agropecuarios — 3, 4, 7,11,12

Market at garden, 7   Bakery, 9

Figure 6.5 Drift showing provisioning activity

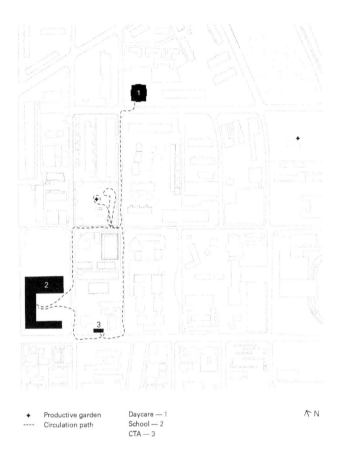

+	Productive garden	Daycare — 1	↑ N
----	Circulation path	School — 2	
		CTA — 3	

School, 2   CTA gives plant advice, 3

Figure 6.6 Drift of school children and their interaction with the garden

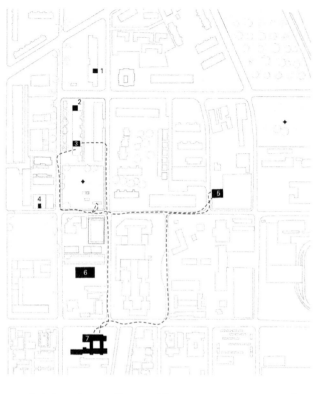

<table>
<tbody>
<tr><td>✦</td><td>Productive garden</td><td>Pharmacy — 1, 5</td><td>↖ N</td></tr>
<tr><td>----</td><td>Circulation path</td><td>Consultorio — 2, 3, 4, 6</td><td></td></tr>
<tr><td></td><td></td><td>Hospital</td><td></td></tr>
<tr><td></td><td></td><td>Polyclinic — 7</td><td></td></tr>
<tr><td></td><td></td><td>House of the grandparents</td><td></td></tr>
</tbody>
</table>

Consultorio, 3

Polyclinic, 7

Figure 6.7 Drift of persons seeking medical treatment

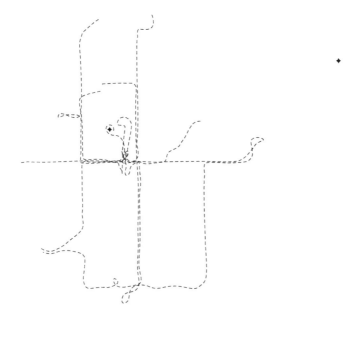

♦   Productive garden   ↖ N
---- Circulation path

Produce being sold at the garden

Figure 6.8 Combined drift activities

- The garden using local organic waste from street cuttings as a component of the compost it uses on the farm. Community members facilitated this with prunings from their properties. Collectively the neighbourhood allocates some of the state-owned street garbage bins specifically for this use. This is an informal community composting programme that is based on local relationships and needs.
- All the people who work in the garden live locally. Several live in the residential units that overlook the garden in the adjacent blocks. This gives people flexibility with their lives as they can come and go during the day. The informal surveillance from these buildings provides after-hours security for La Sazón.
- With limited access to machinery and petrochemicals, the proximity of human labour to this site of urban agriculture is important. Locating farming near housing also reduces the distance from cultivation-to-consumption.
- The garden provides all the employees with produce for their families. This supplements their incomes and provides healthy food.
- Workers' remuneration increases with higher yields and sales. Their business model includes profit sharing with the entire workforce. In most state-run organisations, the employees pilfer from the enterprise but here they all share in the financial success of the company. This profit sharing is in addition to their monthly salary, making it a lucrative employment opportunity, especially with the free food and medicinal supplements that are provided.
- The garden provides free food to local pregnant women, the Sistema de Atención a la Familia, and the casa de los abuelos. Workers deliver this food, thereby leading to positive relationship building between the workers and the recipients within the community.
- Knowledge transfer, through teaching and education, is exchanged daily with the students from the local schools attending the labour education stream of classes and circles of interest.
- La Sazón was the only urban agriculture site among the three case studies that was expanding its operation during the time of the study. While the other two sites were transitioning towards growing more medicinal plants, this farm was actively increasing its supply of fresh produce to the neighbourhood and expanding the footprint of the farm to fill in any leftover spaces between it and the neighbouring buildings. There was also interest in cultivating additional fallow land in the community.
- A meat market was added in 2015, providing diversity to the market's offerings. In 2019 an additional market stall was built, as the farm

wanted more venders to enhance provisioning on this site and make it more convenient for customers.

- The bakery, meat market, and point of sale enhance the quality of this urban space, making this a dynamic hub for provisioning.
- Conversations with customers revealed that both the meat market and the produce from this point of sale are of a very high quality and offer more diversity than the other surrounding markets. Even though it is slightly more expensive, it is the preferred place to shop.
- There was more pedestrian and economic activity in the vegetated streets surrounding the site. These activities had all increased over the duration of the study and these had a direct relationship to each other. When asked, people agreed that the shade and vegetation made it more pleasant to shop there. The care and cultivation of the vegetation directly affected pedestrian and economic activity.
- Information boards had been posted throughout the neighbourhood; these offer education to the population regarding the health benefits of the vegetables and fruits that are available in the markets and on the farm, including the medicinal values of certain fruits and vegetables. These provide informal health education.
- Conviviality was very apparent amongst customers, passers by, neighbours, assistants, and producers. This was enhanced by the shade and the scent of certain plants, and the seating that had been added to the market areas and along the green linkage corridors made this a pleasurable shopping experience.
- While parents shopped, their children played in shady spaces adjacent to the markets and the farms. The children appeared happy to accompany parents on these expeditions as they could explore these hybrid spaces while their parents perused the garden and its offerings.
- Goats and horses grazed on the fallow land surrounding the site (Figure 6.12). This kept the grass short and provided food for the animals. What might have felt like a subversive activity was helpful and sustainable in that it fed the livestock, kept the grass under control, and facilitated recreational use, such as football or baseball.
- State networks supports the site by providing subsidised essentials, including seeds and biological pest control.
- The state facilitates ongoing access to training and information regarding the latest best practices in urban agriculture.
- The state has made the land available to the cooperative in usufruct for 20 years. The use of the land is renewable, based on continuous positive reviews from state inspectors. While these reviews are no doubt stressful for the facility, they serve to improve the operation of the

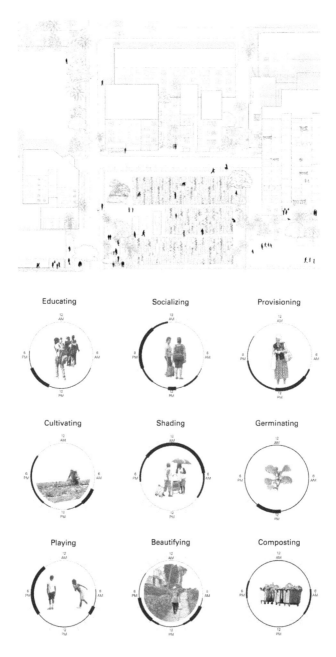

Figure 6.9 Rhythms and networks across the section, 8am–10am

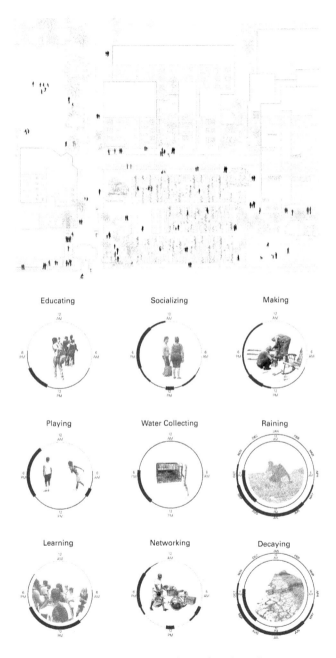

Figure 6.10 Rhythms and networks across the section, 4pm–6pm

place by continually enhancing knowledge and best practices. These state inspections also facilitate knowledge on the diversification of plant species, animal breeds, and the variety in each production unit.

• When state inspectors recognised this garden as successful, it brought pride to the facility and status to the community.

• In a country with enormous state involvement, the producers feel as if they had quite a lot of independence and autonomy in controlling, distributing, and selling the harvest they produce.

• The site's proximity to the university and extensive medical facilities has an impact on the client's requests, especially since the hospital nearby has a teaching centre of natural medicine with a close relationship with this farm.

Urban agriculture involves ingenuity and necessity alongside government support. Construction strategies for planting beds were researched by the state and taught to producers. The Instituto de Investigaciones Fundamentales en Agricultura Tropical (INIFAT) developed the *Manual Técnico para Organopónicos, Huertos Intensivos y Organoponía Semiprotegida*. This book is considered the authority on urban agriculture in Cuba and was produced with the participation of and input from many governmental and academic institutions. It is readily available to citizens digitally and in print. The manual suggests that cultivation sites should be integrated into the aesthetics of the environment in which they are located, and bed construction should facilitate recycling from sites of collapse or use locally available or grown materials. Materials used at La Sazón and the surrounding farms include roofing tiles, siding, masonry, pipes, scrap wood, and bamboo. Several variations are suggested in the manual, along with specifications for the composition of the raised beds in *organopónicos* and planting beds in *huertos intensivos*. In the case of La Sazón, the cultivation beds met the criteria as they were approximately 1.2 m wide, for ease of ergonomic access from both sides. The lengths of the beds did not typically exceed the maximum of 25m to facilitate movement between planted areas. The spaces between the individual beds were approximately 0.5 m wide, with wider passageways of 2–3m between groups of beds to enable harvesting and other work (Figure 6.11). All of this is essential to optimise yields. The beds should be oriented perpendicular to the gradient of the terrain and, optimally, should run from north to south for enhanced sun exposure.[32] This was not possible at La Sazón as this would, according to the producers, have conflicted with the grade and access points into the garden.

6.4.3 Layering

After the 1992 Rio Summit, Fidel Castro adopted an ecological approach to politics that intensified throughout his remaining tenure in office and

A	Group of beds	Growing beds should be oriented perpendicular to the gradient of the terrain.
B	Aisle (2000-3000mm) This space enables harvesting and other work.	Growing beds should run North to South for enhanced sun exposure.
C	Growing bed (1200 mm)	
D	Space between growing beds (500mm)	It is important to add organics to the soil as nutrients.
E	Length of growing beds (15 000-25 000mm)	A supply of compost should be located adjacent to the planting beds.
F	Compost bed	

Figure 6.11 Layout of the garden as recommended by the State

Natalie Copping: View of market, 2019

View of farmers

Horse grazing on fallow land

Figure 6.12 Everyday life showing growing and living surrounding the site

Graphics by Stavros Kondeas, Rita Wang, Alicia McDowell (Gilmore), and Lucas McDowell

deepened even after he stepped down in 2008. The Global Financial Crisis of 2008 further precipitated his environmental fervour, where he always saw '[t]he enemy' as 'constant: the United States and its mortal weapon, capitalism'.[33] Such a mandate was a complete ideological shift in cultivation from the large-scale Soviet model that had dominated the country until 1989. Forced by necessity, the Cuban government hit the reset button during the Special Period and embraced local small-scale organic farming as part of its revolutionary praxis. This bottom-up ecological approach became a new layer that appeared all over the country and was particularly evident in the vicinity of this site. Forestier's vision of a Gran Parque Nacional was in many ways similarly positioned in that it would have consisted of linked parks and plazas throughout the city. It would have created green ribbons from the Malecón to the Loma de los Catalanes, from the Colón Cemetery to the park surrounding the Atarés Castle, and large swaths along the Río Almendares' watershed. It was largely unrealised other than the Bosque de la Habana, an urban forest along the banks of the Río Almendares. However, in this particular neighbourhood, a type of green corridor has appeared within these grassroots farms and vegetated connections that starts to tease out Forestier's intentions for this system of green linkages.

6.4.4 Rhizome

The extended site consists of five urban agriculture locations (Figure 6.1). While most of the research was conducted surrounding La Sazón (Site 1), observations were made around the four other sites. These facilities all have quite different rhythms and the rhizomic activity was evident in the comparison of these sites. Significantly less trading activity takes place at locations 2 and 4. These facilities supply produce to the surrounding government ministries, making their client base very stable, with little competition. The absence of economic activity is reflected in the quality of the point-of-sale market spaces at 2 and 4. They had little produce for sale, only the vegetables that were cultivated that day and superfluous to the ministries' requirements were available for purchase. In addition, they do not partner with other farms. Site 3 shares much in common with site 1 in that it is also associated with another farm in the outskirts of Havana, but the scale of the operation was significantly smaller. The entrepreneurial activity at the site appeared to have improved the urban conditions surrounding it and helped to create strong connections to the community. Site 3, like Site 1, operated outreach programmes with local schools and care homes, and the daily rhythms of the garden were livelier due to these extended networks. Interestingly, Site 5 was closed from 2015 until 2018, but reopened in July 2019 with the depression in the economy.

The other important rhizomic relationships involve the direct connection between vegetation, the presence of shade, sensorial experiences, and heightened economic activity surrounding a site. This might seem to be counterintuitive, but in the lands surrounding Plaza de la Revolución, the shady vegetated routes facilitate high levels of trading activity along with the increase in pedestrian traffic.

6.5 Conclusion

Since urban agriculture was first explored as an official state-supported endeavour in Cuba during the Special Period, the government has developed many resources related to the cultivation of produce within urban centres, which it offers to the population to support the practice. The government recognised the need to specially train agricultural workers in urban areas due to the particular agroecological techniques that are necessary. The opportunities came in many forms, including through post-secondary education, agricultural vocational schools aimed towards training youth, school classes, and extracurricular activities within circles of interest. These activities are all supported at La Sazón. As a result, it has created a system where anyone is able to gather the essential knowledge and, in this part of the city, they can also get access to the land they need to begin producing food close to where they live.

Extending the offerings of this garden to include food markets and having relationships with community groups closes the loop that connects the farm to the table. It also addresses one of the weaknesses of urban agriculture (as outlined in María Caridad Cruz and Roberto Sánchez Medina's book, *Agriculture in the City*) as being the inadequate integration of the productive landscape and the city. Numerous studies show the physical and mental health benefits that are related to implementing greenery within communities. This integration was first recommended by Jean Claude Nicolás Forestier and Martinez Inclan in their master plans, and it is starting to be evident at the community scale in this part of the city. The integration of these fragrant, vegetated, and productive spaces is vital to the community's social, ecological, and economic health. It is also exciting to see that in Plaza de la Revolución, under the watchful eye of the José Martí monument, many of his teachings are now being realised through everyday life in this neighbourhood.

Notes

1. City Population, "City Population".
2. Christopher P. Baker, *Moon Havana* (Berkeley, CA: Avalon Travel, 2018), 81–82.

3. Scarpaci, Segre and Coyula, *Havana: Two Faces of the Antillean Metropolis*, 128.
4. Baker, *Moon Havana*, 81.
5. Pablo Alonso González, "The Organization of Commemorative Space in Postcolonial Cuba: From Civic Square to Square of the Revolution," *Organization* 23, no. 1 (2016): 57.
6. Gold, *People and State in Socialist Cuba: Ideas and Practices of Revolution*, 165.
7. Alonso González, "The Organization of Commemorative Space in Postcolonial Cuba: From Civic Square to Square of the Revolution," 65–67.
8. Staff, "Two Men, the Same Dream," *Granma*, 26 January, 2018, http://en.granma.cu/cuba/2018-01-26/two-men-the-same-dream (accessed 7 February 2018).
9. Gold, *People and State in Socialist Cuba: Ideas and Practices of Revolution*, 113.
10. Gold, *People and State in Socialist Cuba: Ideas and Practices of Revolution*, 87.
11. Eduardo Luis Rodríguez, *The Havana Guide: Modern Architecture 1925–1965* (New York: Princeton Architectural Press, 2000), 173–185.
12. Lefebvre, *The Production of Space*, 167.
13. Gold, *People and State in Socialist Cuba: Ideas and Practices of Revolution*, 74.
14. Lynch, *What Time Is This Place?*, 28.
15. Lynch, *What Time Is This Place?*, 28.
16. Gold, *People and State in Socialist Cuba: Ideas and Practices of Revolution*, 71.
17. Ministerio de Educación de Cuba (MINED), "Programas De Estudio," www.mined.gob.cu/ (accessed March 2018).
18. Ministerio de Educación de Cuba (MINED), "Programas De Estudio."
19. Koont, *Sustainable Urban Agriculture in Cuba*, 86.
20. Ministerio de Educación de Cuba (MINED), "Programas De Estudio."
21. Denise F. Blum, *Cuban Youth and Revolutionary Values: Educating the New Socialist Citizen* (Austin: University of Texas Press, 2012), 8.
22. Blum, *Cuban Youth and Revolutionary Values: Educating the New Socialist Citizen*, 11.
23. Katie Bucher, *Sowing City Schools: Teachers and Garden Education in Havana and Philadelphia*, eds. Heidi A. Ross et al. (Ann Arbor: ProQuest Dissertations Publishing, 2012), 147.
24. Blum, *Cuban Youth and Revolutionary Values: Educating the New Socialist Citizen*, 151.
25. EcuRed, "Casa de Abuelos," www.ecured.cu/Casa_de_Abuelos (accessed 2018).
26. Instituto de Geografía, *Atlas Nacional De Cuba, En El Décimo Aniversario De La Revolución* (La Habana: Academia de Ciencias de Cuba, 1970).
27. Jean-Francois Lejeune, John Beusterien and Narciso G. Menocal, "The City as Landscape: Jean Claude Nicolas Forestier and the Great Urban Works of Havana, 1925–1930," *The Journal of Decorative and Propaganda Arts* 22 (1996): 168.
28. Lejeune, Beusterien and Menocal, "The City as Landscape: Jean Claude Nicolas Forestier and the Great Urban Works of Havana, 1925–1930," 153.
29. McDonough, "Situationist Space," 65.
30. Debord, "Theory of the Dérive."
31. McDonough, "Situationist Space," 65.
32. INIFAT, Instituto de Investigaciones Fundamentales en Agricultura Tropical, ed., *Manual Técnico Para Organopónicos, Huertos Intensivos Y Organoponía Semiprotegida*, Seventh ed. (La Habana: INIFAT, 2010), 16.
33. Gold, *People and State in Socialist Cuba: Ideas and Practices of Revolution*, 114.

7 Reflections

7.1 Introduction

Urban agriculture is highly dependent upon the specific context of the place and the needs of the citizens. It has the potential to allow people to have a visceral connection to cultivation and nature, it improves their diet, counteracts food scarcity, and helps them achieve food sovereignty. All of these factors contributed to the success of these gardens within Cuba. In addition, urban agriculture has encouraged citizens, with the support of the government both nationally and locally, to participate in grassroots governance surrounding these sites and to bolster community events, where people come together to celebrate and learn about food. These gardens have strong synergies with other institutions, including healthcare and education as well as infrastructures—such as water and waste management—making them part of circular economies and ecologies within the city. It is the broad reach of these sites of urban agriculture and their capacity to engage citizens with cultural and social activities surrounding growing that makes them important to study for consideration in the future of the city. In this way, urban agriculture in Cuba might be seen as unique, as these networks and connections are intimately intertwined with each other and are closer to the original definition of 'agriculture' in that they involve caring and culture.

From my first visit to Havana in 2011 and progressively throughout the study, I suspected that these sites of urban agriculture were different to what I had observed in other countries. While urban farming certainly achieved many of these goals in other parts of the world, it was the infiltration of these gardens into everyday community life that was so specific within Cuba. These farms were linked to numerous other networks and rhythms that involved wellness, research, spirituality, community, and economic activities; more than I had ever imagined at the onset of this study. However, these networks and rhythms were so subtle—place, people, and time dependent—they were impossible to see, especially during a brief interaction with a garden during an

DOI: 10.4324/9781003201410-7

occasional visit. What was required was a disciplined method to observe and record everyday occurrences to understand these spaces. Rhythmanalysis and the series of tactics employed, including drift, rhizome, layering, and game-board, emerged as a way of observing and recording these sites over time.

7.2 Reflections on the Methodology as a Design Method

Reflections on the methodology are important as they suggest future ways of using this incipient conceptual framework and especially how it might be used to inform design work. Firstly, it is an iterative and time-consuming process that employs different tactics that were apposite at different points throughout the progression of the work. It was also an active process whereby the researcher somehow becomes a 'cultural intermediary or broker'.[1] It was necessary to be deeply connected to the place. Rather than floating over the city to find content, rhythmanalysis enmeshes the person within the study as the researcher's own rhythms become intimately entangled with the place. Rather than bringing ideas from away and imposing them on a place, such a study requires that one learn from being part of the specificity of the place. Through such a process, one becomes invested in and empathetic to the culture. Concurrently, distance also plays a crucial part in the approach as the researcher moves from being extremely close and embedded within the place to reviewing and considering the rhythms from a distance. The ability to reflect on the rhythms away from the intensity of the study increases the capability to be thoughtful about the work and to use it as a tool for design. Lefebvre described both the near and far analyses as being part of the process.

Lefebvre's unfinished work on rhythmanalysis was the starting point for this research. Recording and documenting the rhythms enabled this novel methodology to become an interactive design process; it is a system of simul-taneously 'finding' and 'founding' that is intimately enmeshed in the place.[2] Lefebvre's definition of rhythms is important to keep reiterating as it is easy to imagine a more scientific description rather than one involving the broad and nuanced interaction of people and place. The different tactics employed to uncover these everyday rhythms were useful in recognising the diverse beats of a place, with the real power being that they can inform the design work in a community. While one might think that using this method continu-ally produces designs that are more or less the same (having been generated from similar findings within the place), it in fact leverages radical and previ-ously unseen relationships through the different mapping processes. Drift highlights patterns of movement, limits, extents, and psychogeographical readings of a place. It uncovers the everyday lived experiences. Layering is the most familiar of the methods and is a good starting point. It juxta-poses different discovered patterns, often incorporating traces of history, and serves as a predictive tool for the future city. Specific programmes within a community are revealed through layering along with adjacencies and neighbourhood features. The game-board highlights the symbiotic relationships that exist within communities. It reveals networks and possibilities. These associations are discovered between both human and non-human actors as it reveals the lived experiences of a place. Rhizome is enigmatic and takes time to understand. It uncovers how seemingly unrelated influences are important within a place and has a tremendous power to reveal unseen potentialities (See Figure 2.3). While it is impossible to start with rhizome mapping, it is an important contribution to the work. It may be that the full opportunities of rhizomes within the work have yet to be revealed. In addition, it may be that all four methods are not necessary or that there is redundancy in the overlap. However, in many ways it was the iterative teasing out of all these rhythms through the different mapping methods that revealed so much about a place and that holds such promise as a method for design.

There are certainly weaknesses to such a method. For one thing, the process partially depends on serendipity as to what you might uncover on each visit. As has been said before, it is also highly time consuming and requires multiple visits over an extended period. Without the ongoing discipline and the correct amount of time allocated to a study, it is easy to jump to conclusions about a place from a single interaction. It also requires building trust within the community to understand the linkages and networks surrounding a site as some of the rhythms are subversive and can take a long time to uncover. While the method clearly gives content for design (through programme and materiality), there is ultimately a jump or translation needed as the process transitions from recording and documenting rhythms into design.

It has also been suggested that any location might serve as a study site in Havana and that the urban agriculture was not actually necessary. This is partially true—I could certainly have performed the same research on schools or bakeries and many of the findings would have been similar—however it is the polyrhythmia of these gardens, the intensity of both linear and cyclical rhythms colliding within one place, that made these gardens particularly potent as the study site.

There are certainly more automated systems that could be used for recording the life of a city, but it would have been difficult and perhaps impossible to organise this in Cuba. This is a country where foreigners are viewed with suspicion; researchers need to be vetted to obtain visas to do their work; internet access is expensive and slow; GPS equipment (and anything else unusual) is prone to be seized by customs; sketchbooks and cameras are searched by state police; and meticulous records are kept on everyone and anything entering and leaving the country. Low technology is required for any study method in Cuba and, in keeping with the aspirations for the research, it was vital to be present and curious within and around the study sites, immersed in the everyday life of the city.

This process is especially useful for understanding sites and places that are culturally unfamiliar. However, it also uncovers hidden potentials within what might be considered familiar territory. While each of the mapping methods is understood as revealing the unseen possibilities of a place, turning it into a type of temporal mapping over time makes it particularly effective for teasing out information. So often our understanding of space as designers is from a distance and involves a brief interaction with a place over a short span of time. Measuring the quotidian life of a place over several years reveals patterns and networks previously unimagined both for local and distant researchers.

Rhythmanalysis is an incipient creative urban research method that has the ability to tease out information about the city—particularly the importance of its everyday life—to shape both our current understanding and the potential for future urban transformation and architecture. The temporal aspect to this method is important as it monitors change in the city, both subtle and profound, that can turn the qualitative research into quantitative design data.

7.2.1 Rhythms of Research

Rather than staying in Havana for an extended study period, my research occurred incrementally and was divided into regular short visits of one to four weeks, spread over six years. This had its own inherent rhythm of going to and returning from Havana and, with each trip, learning from the previous encounter. The changes seemed more salient with this temporal method of study, as the recordings that were taken at intervals over a six-year period showed far more variance than would be evident within a single extended stay of several months.

Coming into this study as a mother, an architect, and a part-time assistant professor each revealed quite different encounters and timescales with the city that might not have been so apparent to another researcher. The passage of time, as a parent, followed the ages of my children. Children that often accompanied me in my studies. The presence of children is certainly less threatening, as a researcher this often led to the breaking down of barriers as people readily discussed the shared experience of parenting that seems to transcend culture. Intimate understandings of activities, such as daycare and schooling, became common ground for conversations. With children in tow, I was often invited into facilities (such as schools, daycares, homes for pregnant women, and houses for grandparents) that might otherwise have been less welcoming to a childless researcher. Seeing things through the eyes of a child, and hearing their opinions was also a perspective that many researchers never encounter.

7.2.2 Cuba's Timescales

Since the Sixth Communist Party Congress in spring 2011, the government has introduced reforms legalising house sales and expanding self-employment, incrementally moving Cuba towards a freer market economy. In 2016, Fidel Castro, the protagonist of the Cuban Revolution, died. Over his life, he inextricably changed the rhythms for each Cuban and any person who had been intimately involved with the country.

The reinstatement of embassies in Havana and Washington and the evolving USA presidencies have had impacts on the rhythms of this city. Barack Obama's thawing of diplomatic relations and his visit in 2016 were game changers in terms of easing years of hostilities. As the city started to ready itself for the impending influx of American tourists in 2017, Donald Trump rolled back the advancements. As of yet, and with the complications of the covid-19 pandemic, Joe Biden's policies are not fully known. However, with the progressive opening up of self-employment, entrepreneurial activities have become increasingly innovative with evolving businesses continually popping up. Typically, to service the tourist industry, these companies are every bit as sophisticated as elsewhere in the world. However, alongside this economic energy, the government often makes sweeping changes across the country, rolling back licensures for certain practices or businesses that had previously been permitted. In Havana, as quickly as people became successful, they can be suppressed; as the rules change, they are again forced to adapt. In 2019, the economy collapsed, and the country returned to some of the same conditions that had prevailed during the Special Period. The covid-19 pandemic has furthered this recession and, along with country wide protests, sites of urban agriculture have ramped up production and have again become more prevalent throughout the country.

Underlying all these changes and rhythms is a sense of fine balance—imposed by the government and society—that encompasses maintaining socialism and all that the Revolution fought for and upheld, alongside trying to bolster the Cuban economy and freedom. All of these temporal events are manifested in the lives of the citizens through the interstices of everyday life. These sites are an intricate blend of social, natural, cultural, political, and economic practices, all of which are both provisional and cumulative, but rhythmanalysis is stealthy and has the power to uncover it all.

7.3 Final Thoughts

These sites of urban agriculture in Havana are continually evolving, with the changes mirroring many of the shifts that have taken place within the country locally, nationally, and globally. While this study in Cuba could have been done surrounding any type of space, these sites have a particularly pivotal relationship with everyday life, as they exhibit a multitude of linear and cyclical rhythms that link them to work, exchange, health, education, societal interactions, infrastructure, and climate. While other methodologies and investigations might have yielded similar knowledge, the complexity of the colliding rhythms within and surrounding these gardens makes the study particularly salient. In addition, while one could easily imagine such sites losing relevance within an evolving Cuba, they appear to be recreating themselves and presenting new possibilities for urban life. Rather than being static, these gardens are part of the evolving everyday cultures and rhythms within the city. Here urban agriculture bridges between multiple worlds as it brings the rural into the urban, the visceral into the sanitised, and the highly local into the global—involving human interactions that turn the growing of food into a productive and social activity. So, while the practice of urban agriculture is often highly temporary, it is an important societal occurrence shaping the country.

What was once about survival and access to nutrients is now a preference for local organic produce, which Cubans increasingly consider to be healthier. Embraced by the Western world as a sign of modernity, organic is becoming fashionable among Cubans. Alongside the promotion of agroecological produce, farm-to-table restaurants have started popping up in parts of the city (La Cocina de Esteban and Mediterráneo in Vedado are considered two of the most renowned restaurants in the city). Mediterráneo is affiliated with the local farm Finca Vista Hermosa, which is located in the Guanabacoa neighbourhood of Havana. This urban farm provides provisions that are crafted into fresh, delicious food. While most other restaurants follow exactly the same practices of using local food out of availability and necessity, these restaurants actively advertise this practice. Rooted within many of the ideals of the Slow Food movement, these restaurants promote access to enjoyable food that is nutritious, support cooperative business models, and practice ecological farming. In addition, these farm and restaurant combinations promote agritourism and cultural exchanges through visits to these farms. They also enhance culinary education to help foster an understanding of Cubanidad—Cuban culture through food-centred activities that strengthen local identity.[3]

Green medicine was once considered a poor substitute for allopathic drugs, but it is now seamlessly integrated into the healthcare system through both education and practice. Pharmacies stock as many homeopathic remedies as they do conventional medicines. Food markets throughout the city advertise the health benefits of fruits and vegetables on detailed display boards interspersed amongst the stalls. Discussions with Cuban students and their professors suggested that citizens have knowledge about and use green medicines alongside allopathic treatments. The medical system has addressed this use by educating health practitioners and the population on the benefits and dangers surrounding green medicine.

The practice of teaching school children about cultivation as part of José Martí's thinking began to lose popularity during the 1980s but it resurged after the crisis of the Special Period. Whether this change was political or due to the climate crisis, the result is that there is a broad knowledge about ecological farming practices and the country is always in a state of readiness for the next disaster that jeopardises its food security or sovereignty. Voluntary community service is encouraged. In fact, it is mandatory for students after graduating from university to engage in it to reimburse the state for the free education they have received. This often involves working on a farm and so ecological agriculture is part of the education system at multiple levels and has become embedded in the culture of the country.

In the practice of Afro-Cuban religions, plants represent the origin of all life sources. With a participation rate approaching 70% of the population, for most Cuban citizens these Afro-Cuban religions are part of everyday life. Devoted practice requires multiple interactions with vegetation as many advocates of these religions employ plants 'to worship their symbols and invoke their virtues'; they also use plants for everyday health and spirituality. Access to urban agricultural sites facilitates easy access to growing, and not pre-cut, spiritual plants in the centre of the city. This is particularly important as people have limited mobility to access vegetated spaces. Whether or not one is a believer is immaterial as the Afro-Cuban culture is embodied within these sites and is practised throughout daily life.[4]

This method contributes to both practice and research beyond Cuba. While clearly a method to build knowledge about specific sites within any community, rhythmanalysis along with the mapping methods enables designers and researchers to be more precise about what they observe within a neighbourhood. It gives a clear method to describe both the tangible and intangible assets of a place. As the different mapping methods are rooted within conventional techniques, already used by architects, planners, and urban designers, they are easily accessible and replicable. However, this method of research requires effort—many visits at different times of the day and year and lingering within a place—it necessitates study, accountability, and empathy with a community. These are all attributes that should be important to any design or research project but are often overlooked due to time constraints. It also offers clear opportunities for pre- and post-evaluation of the rhythms of a place that would make researchers, developers, and designers more mindful of and responsible to the everyday life of a community that their work affects.

Rhythmanalysis serves as a research and design tool that helps make places, processes, and people visible. It acknowledges that sites are always involved in the process of making and re-making—a state to which I now realise they (or anything else) will never ultimately arrive. However, these sites have particularity at a moment, defined by specific rhythms and flows that are inextricably linked to place. Without studying the everyday life surrounding these sites, it would be impossible to understand the complexity and assets of the evolving sites and activities. This study makes a strong case for using rhythmanalysis as both a research and design tool for observing and recording rhythms; representing and understanding them through mapping; unpacking the important rhythms; and using them within the next iteration of becoming or founding. Such a design process is inevitably human-centred and includes ecological, economic, and social values. The grass roots beats of a community are heard quietly at first and then rise up, and within this study of quotidian practices they resound more loudly. Such a method reveals that everyday life is far from mundane—it is profound, beautiful, and revolutionary.

Notes

1. Diébédo Francis Kéré, *Francis Kéré: Radically Simple*, eds. Andres Lepik and Ayça Beygo (München: Hatje Cantz, 2016), 173.
2. Corner, *The Landscape Imagination: Collected Essays of James Corner, 1990–2010*, 197.
3. Slow Food International, www.slowfood.com/ (accessed 27 October 2018).
4. Claudia Acevedo, *Orishas: Cuban Syncretism and Spirituality* (Panama City: Aurelia Ediciones, 2018), 1–5.

Glossary

Acopio: state institution that collects and re-distributes food from farms at a controlled price for use by the population

Barbacoa: informal and often illegal mezzanines added to dwellings

Bodega: store providing ration book food, found on most blocks in the city

Carnicería: butcher, often part of rationing network

Casa de los abuelos: house of the grandparents, daycare facility for the elderly

Ciudadelas: multi-unit residence consisting of a single or double row of rooms constructed along a courtyard. These rooms often house entire families.

Comités de Defensa de la Revolución (CDR): Committee for the Defense of the Revolution

Consultorios del Médico de la Familia: community doctor's office

Consultorios Tiendas Agropecuarios (CTA): government-run plant information kiosks often selling seedlings and tools

Cuarterías: large house subdivided into rooms

Cubanidad: the essence of being Cuban, evolves over time, and involves culture and food

Cuentapropista: self-employed

Libreta de Abastecimiento: rationing book giving access to highly subsidised food, the actual food products change over time

Lineamientos: guidelines, laws

Mercados Agropecuarios: farmers or agricultural markets

Medicina tradicional: traditional and natural medicine

Parceleros: small-scale farmers

Partido Comunista de Cuba: Communist Party of Cuba

Punto de venta: point-of-sale market often at sites of urban agriculture

Sistema de Atención a la Familia (SAF): cafeterias supplying highly subsidised food to at risk groups of the population

Solar/es: term to reference residential buildings subdivided into single rooms that now serve as housing for families, typically with shared amenities including bathrooms, kitchen, and laundry

Talleres de Transformación Integral de Barrio: Workshops for the Integral Transformation of the Neighbourhood

Bibliography

Abrahams, Harlan. *Raul Castro and the New Cuba: A Close-Up View of Change*, Edited by Arturo Lopez-Levy. Jefferson: McFarland & Co., 2011.

Abrams, Janet, and Peter Hall. *Else/Where: Mapping New Cartographies of Networks and Territories*. Minneapolis: University of Minnesota Design Institute, 2006.

Acevedo, Claudia. *Orishas: Cuban Syncretism and Spirituality*. Panama City: Aurelia Ediciones, 2018.

Alonso González, Pablo. "The Organization of Commemorative Space in Postcolonial Cuba: From Civic Square to Square of the Revolution." *Organization* 23, no. 1 (2016): 47–70.

Altieri, Miguel, Nelso Companioni, Kristina Cañizares, Catherine Murphy, Peter Rosset, Martin Bourque, and Clara Nicholls. "The Greening of the 'Barrios': Urban Agriculture for Food Security in Cuba." *Agriculture and Human Values* 16, no. 2 (1999): 131–140.

Amin, Ash, and Stephen Graham. "The Ordinary City." *Transactions of the Institute of British Geographers* 22, no. 4 (1997): 411–429.

Amin, Ash, and Nigel Thrift. *Cities: Reimagining the Urban*. Cambridge: Polity, 2002.

Anguelovski, Isabelle. *Neighborhood as Refuge Community Reconstruction, Place Remaking, and Environmental Justice in the City*. Cambridge: MIT Press, 2014.

Aravena Mori, Alejandro. *Elemental: Manual De Vivienda Incremental Y Diseño Participativo/Incremental Housing and Participatory Design Manual*, Edited by Andrés Iacobelli. Ostfildern: Hatje, 2012.

Arrechea Jiménez, Alejandro. "Dirección Provincial de Planificación Física Ciudad de La Habana." Talk presented to Dalhousie University Havana Studio, Havana, Cuba, October 5, 2015.

August, Arnold. *Cuba and Its Neighbours: Democracy in Motion*. Halifax: Fernwood, 2013.

Baker, Christopher P. *Moon Havana*. Berkeley, CA: Avalon Travel, 2018.

Barthel, Stephan, and Christian Isendahl. "Urban Gardens, Agriculture, and Water Management: Sources of Resilience for Long-Term Food Security in Cities." *Ecological Economics* 86 (2013): 224–234.

Barthes, Roland. *How to Live Together: Novelistic Simulations of Some Everyday Spaces*. New York: Columbia University Press, 2013.

Bhatia, Neeraj, and Lateral Office. *Coupling: Strategies for Infrastructural Opportunism*. New York: Princeton Architectural Press, 2011.

Birkenmaier, Anke, and Esther Katheryn Whitfield. *Havana beyond the Ruins: Cultural Mappings after 1989*. Durham: Duke University Press, 2011.

Blum, Denise F. *Cuban Youth and Revolutionary Values: Educating the New Socialist Citizen*. Austin: University of Texas Press, 2012.

Borden, Iain. *Skateboarding, Space and the City: Architecture and the Body*. New York: Berg, 2001.

Brandon, George. "The Uses of Plants in Healing in an Afro-Cuban Religion, Santeria." *Journal of Black Studies* 22, no. 1 (1991): 55–76.

Brenner, Neil, ed. *Implosions/Explosions: Towards a Study of Planetary Urbanization*. Berlin: Jovis, 2014.

Brook, Richard. *Urban Maps: Instruments of Narrative and Interpretation in the City*, Edited by Nick Dunn. Farnham: Ashgate, 2011.

Brotherton, Pierre Sean. *Revolutionary Medicine: Health and the Body in Post-Soviet Cuba*. Durham: Duke University Press, 2012.

Bucher, Katie. *Sowing City Schools: Teachers and Garden Education in Havana and Philadelphia*, Edited by Heidi A. Ross, William Corsaro, Barbara Dennis, Bradley Levinson and Margaret Sutton. Ann Arbor: ProQuest Dissertations Publishing, 2012.

Bunschoten, Raoul, and Chora. *Urban Flotsam: Stirring the City*. Rotterdam: 010 Publishers, 2001.

Burman, Mary E., and Audrey M. Kleinsasser. "Ethical Guidelines for Use of Student Work: Moving from Teaching's Invisibility to Inquiry's Visibility in the Scholarship of Teaching and Learning." *The Journal of General Education* 53, no. 1 (2004): 59–79.

Carmona, Matthew, ed. *Explorations in Urban Design: An Urban Design Research Primer*. Farnham: Ashgate, 2014.

Chase, John, Margaret Crawford, and John Kaliski. *Everyday Urbanism*. New York: Monacelli Press, 1999.

Chateloin, Felicia. "Una Mirada a La Historia Urbana De Centro Habana: La Necesidad Del Reconocimiento." In *Centro Habana: Un Futuro Sustentable*, edited by Gina Rey, 28–34. La Habana: Facultad de Arquitectura de La Universidad de La Habana, 2009.

Chen, Yi. *Practising Rhythmanalysis: Theories and Methodologies*. London: Rowman & Littlefield International, 2017.

City Population. "City Population." www.citypopulation.de/en/cuba/admin/ (accessed April 2021).

Clouse, Carey. *Farming Cuba: Urban Agriculture from the Ground Up*. New York: Princeton Architectural Press, 2014.

Corbett, Ben. *This Is Cuba: An Outlaw Culture Survives*. Cambridge: Westview Press, 2002.

Corner, James. *The Landscape Imagination: Collected Essays of James Corner, 1990–2010*, Edited by Alison Bick Hirsch. New York: Princeton Architectural Press, 2014.

———. *Recovering Landscape: Essays in Contemporary Landscape Architecture*. New York: Princeton Architectural Press, 1999.

———. "Terra Fluxus." In *The Landscape Urbanism Reader*, edited by Charles Waldheim. New York: Princeton Architectural Press, 2006.

Corrales, Javier. "Cuba's 'Equity without Growth' Dilemma and the 2011 *Lineamientos.*" *LAPS Latin American Politics and Society* 54, no. 3 (2012): 157–184.

Coyula, Mario, and Jill Hamberg. *Understanding Slums: The Case of Havana, Cuba.* Cambridge: David Rockefeller Center for Latin American Studies, 2004.

Cruz, María Caridad, and Roberto Sánchez Medina. *Agriculture in the City a Key to Sustainability in Havana, Cuba.* Kingston: Ian Randle Publishers, 2003.

Debord, Guy. "Theory of the Dérive." *Bureau of Public Secrets.* www.bopsecrets. org/SI/2.derive.htm (accessed May 2016).

de Certeau, Michel. *The Practice of Everyday Life* [L'Invention du Quotidien], Translated by Steven Rendall. Minneapolis: University of Minnesota Press, 1998.

Deleuze, Gilles, and Félix Guattari. *A Thousand Plateaus: Capitalism and Schizophrenia*, Translated by Brian Massumi. London: Continuum, 2004.

del Real, Patricio, and Anna Cristina Pertierra. "Inventar: Recent Struggles and Inventions in Housing in Two Cuban Cities." *Buildings & Landscapes: Journal of the Vernacular Architecture Forum* 15 (2008): 78–92.

Díaz, Gisela, Ana Ma. de la Peña, and Alfonso Alfonso. "Learning from the Past: The Traditional Compact City in Hot-Humid Climates." PLEA 2006: The 23rd Conference on Passive and Low Energy Architecture, Geneva, Switzerland, September 6–8, 2006.

Diener, Roger, and Institut Stadt der Gegenwart. *Switzerland: An Urban Portrait.* Basel: Birkhäuser, 2006.

Dodd, George. *The Food of London: A Sketch of the Chief Varieties, Sources of Supply, Probable Quantities, Modes of Arrival, Processes of Manufacture, Suspected Adulteration, and Machinery of Distribution of the Food for a Community of Two Millions and a Half.* London: Longman, Brown, Green, and Longmans, 1856.

Dubinsky, Karen. *Cuba beyond the Beach: Stories of Life in Havana.* Toronto: Between the Lines, 2016.

EcuRed. www.ecured.cu/

Edensor, Tim. *Geographies of Rhythm Nature, Place, Mobilities and Bodies.* Farnham: Ashgate, 2010.

Engler, Mira, and Center for American Places. *Designing America's Waste Landscapes.* Baltimore: J. Hopkins University Press, 2004.

Erdi Lelandais, Gülçin, ed. *Understanding the City: Henri Lefebvre and Urban Studies.* Newcastle upon Tyne: Cambridge Scholars Publishing, 2014.

Espinosa Lloréns, Ma, Matilde López Torres, Haydee Álvarez, Alexis Pellón Arrechea, Jorge Alejandro García, Susana Díaz Aguirre, and Alejandro Fernández. "Characterization of Municipal Solid Waste from the Main Landfills of Havana City." *Waste Management* 28, no. 10 (2008): 2013–2021.

Fernandez, Ariadna D., and Leonora Angeles. "Building Better Communities: Gender and Urban Regeneration in Cayo Hueso, Havana, Cuba." *Women's Studies International Forum* 32, no. 2 (2009): 80–88.

Fisher, Daniel. "Cuba Opening Could Reopen Fight over Billions in Seized Property." *Forbes*, 2014, sec. Finance.

French, Charles. "The Social Production of Community Garden Space: Case Studies of Boston, Massachusetts and Havana, Cuba." PhD, Durham University of New Hampshire, 2008.

Funes, Fernando. *Sustainable Agriculture and Resistance: Transforming Food Production in Cuba*. Oakland: Food First Books, 2002.

García, Guadalupe. *Beyond the Walled City: Colonial Exclusion in Havana*. Oakland: University of California Press, 2016.

García-Huidobro, Fernando. *Time Builds!: The Experimental Housing Project (PREVI), Lima: Genesis and Outcome* [*¡El Tiempo Construye!: El Proyecto Experimental De Vivienda (PREVI) De Lima: Génesis Y Desenlace*], Edited by Diego Torres Torriti. Barcelona: G. Gili, 2008.

Gehl, Jan. *How to Study Public Life*, Edited by Birgitte Svarre. Washington, DC: Island Press, 2013.

Gold, Marina. *People and State in Socialist Cuba: Ideas and Practices of Revolution*. New York: Palgrave Macmillan US, 2015.

———. "Urban Gardens: Private Property or the Ultimate Socialist Experience?" In *Cuban Intersections of Literary and Urban Spaces*, edited by Carlo Riobó. Albany: State University of New York Press, 2011.

Hamberg, Jill. "Cuba Opens to Private Housing But Preserves Housing Rights." *Race, Poverty & the Environment* 19, no. 1 (2012): 71–74.

Harvey, David. *Justice, Nature, and the Geography of Difference*. Malden: Blackwell Publishers, 1996.

———. *Rebel Cities: From the Right to the City to the Urban Revolution*. London: Verso, 2012.

Havana the New Art of Making Ruins. Directed by Florian Borchmeyer, Matthias Hentschler and Peter Lohmeyer. Global Films, 2010.

Hechevarria-Driggs, Mario. "A New Collapse in Havana." *Cubalog.Eu*. http://cubalog.eu/2016/02/a-new-collapse-in-havana/ (accessed 23 June 2018).

Hernández, Felipe, Peter Kellett, and Lea Allen. *Rethinking the Informal City: Critical Perspectives from Latin America*. New York: Berghahn Books, 2010.

Highmore, Ben. *Cityscapes: Cultural Readings in the Material and Symbolic City*. Basingstoke: Palgrave Macmillan, 2005.

Holston, James. *Insurgent Citizenship: Disjunctions of Democracy and Modernity in Brazil*. Princeton: Princeton University Press, 2008.

Humboldt, Alexander von. *The Island of Cuba*, Edited by John Sidney Thrasher. New York: Negro Universities Press, 1969.

INIFAT, Instituto de Investigaciones Fundamentales en Agricultura Tropical, ed. *Manual Técnico Para Organopónicos, Huertos Intensivos Y Organoponía Semiprotegida*. Seventh ed. La Habana: INIFAT, 2010.

———. "Los Consultorios-Tiendas Del Agricultor, Una Opción Cada Vez Más Viable Para Los Productores." www.ausc.co.cu/index.php/72-los-consultorios-tiendas-del-agricultor-una-opcion-cada-vez-mas-viable-para-los-productores (accessed December 2018).

Iñiguez, Luisa. *Las Tantas Habanas: Estrategias Para Comprender Sus Dinámicas Sociales*. Ciencias Sociales Y Humanidades. La Habana: Editorial UH, 2014.

Instituto de Geografía. *Atlas Nacional De Cuba, En El Décimo Aniversario De La Revolución*. La Habana: Academia de Ciencias de Cuba, 1970.

International Cooperative Alliance. "What Is a Cooperative?" www.ica.coop/en (accessed January 2019).

Jacobs, Jane. *The Death and Life of Great American Cities*. New York: Random House, 2002.

Jacobs, Jane, Samuel Zipp, and Nathan Storring. *Vital Little Plans: The Short Works of Jane Jacobs*. New York: Random House, 2016.

Kent, James Clifford. "Walker Evans's Psychogeographic Mapping of Havana, 1933." *History of Photography* 37, no. 3 (2013): 326–340.

Kéré, Diébédo Francis. *Francis Kéré: Radically Simple*, Edited by Andres Lepik and Ayça Beygo. München: Hatje Cantz, 2016.

Koont, Sinan. *Sustainable Urban Agriculture in Cuba*. Contemporary Cuba. Gainesville: University Press of Florida, 2011.

Körner, I., I. Saborit-Sánchez, and Y. Aguilera-Corrales. "Proposal for the Integration of Decentralised Composting of the Organic Fraction of Municipal Solid Waste into the Waste Management System of Cuba." *Waste Management* 28, no. 1 (2008): 64–72.

Kumaraswami, Par. *Rethinking the Cuban Revolution Nationally and Regionally: Politics, Culture and Identity*. Chichester: Wiley-Blackwell, 2012.

Kurlansky, Mark. *Havana: A Subtropical Delirium*. London: Bloomsbury, 2017.

Laffita, Rojas O. "Materiales De Construcción, Ese Delicado Asunto: La Corrupción Mina Toda La Industria." *Cubanet*. www.cubanet.org/actualidad-destacados/materiales-de-construccion-ese-delicado-asunto/ (accessed January 2018).

Leatherbarrow, David. *Architecture Oriented Otherwise*. New York: Princeton Architectural Press, 2009.

Lefebvre, Henri. *Critique of Everyday Life*. London: Verso, 1991a.

———. *The Production of Space* [La production de l'Espace], Translated by Donald Nicholson-Smith. Oxford: Blackwell, 1991b.

———. *Rhythmanalysis: Space, Time and Everyday Life*, Translated by Stuart Elden and Gerald Moore. London: Continuum, 2004.

———. *The Urban Revolution*. Minneapolis: University of Minnesota Press, 2003.

Lefebvre, Henri, Stuart Elden, Elizabeth Lebas, and Eleonore Kofman. *Henri Lefebvre*. New York: Continuum, 2003.

Lefebvre, Henri, John Moore, and Gregory Elliott. *Critique of Everyday Life*. London: Verso, 2014.

Lehtovuori, Panu, and Hille Koskela. "From Momentary to Historic: Rhythms in the Social Production of Urban Space, the Case of Calçada De Sant'Ana, Lisbon." *Sociological Review* 61 (2013): 124–143.

Leitgeb, Friedrich, Sarah Schneider, and Christian Vogl. "Increasing Food Sovereignty with Urban Agriculture in Cuba." *Agriculture and Human Values* 33, no. 2 (2016): 415–426.

Lejeune, Jean-François. *Cruelty & Utopia: Cities and Landscapes of Latin America*. New York: Princeton Architectural Press, 2005.

Lejeune, Jean-Francois, John Beusterien, and Narciso G. Menocal. "The City as Landscape: Jean Claude Nicolas Forestier and the Great Urban Works of Havana, 1925–1930." *The Journal of Decorative and Propaganda Arts* 22 (1996): 150–185.

Lévi-Strauss, Claude. *The Savage Mind.* Chicago: University of Chicago Press, 1966.

Lickwar, Phoebe, and Roxi Thoren. *Farmscape: The Design of Productive Landscapes.* New York: Routledge, 2020.

Lydon, Maeve, ed. *Mapping Our Common Ground a Community and Green Mapping Resource Guide.* Victoria: Common Ground, 2007.

Lynch, Kevin. *The Image of the City.* Cambridge: MIT Press, 1960.

———. *What Time Is This Place?* Cambridge: MIT Press, 1972.

Marx, Gary. "Getting One's Way on an Isle of Want." *Chicago Tribune*, November 15, 2004, sec. Letter from Havana.

Massey, Doreen B. *For Space.* London: Sage, 2005.

McDonough, Thomas F. "Situationist Space." *October* 67 (1994): 59–77.

Meyer, Kurt. "Rhythms, Streets, Cities." In *Space, Difference, Everyday Life: Reading Henri Lefebvre*, translated by Bandulasena Goonewardena, edited by Kanishka Goonewardena. New York: Routledge, 2008.

Ministerio de Educación de Cuba (MINED). "Programas De Estudio." www.mined.gob.cu/ (accessed March 2018).

Ministerio de Salud Pública. *Ministerio De Salud Pública Resolución Ministerial No. 381.* La Habana: La República de Cuba Ministerio de Justicia, 2015.

Miroff, Nick. "A Socialist Vision Fades in Cuba's Biggest Housing Project." *The Washington Post*, December 29, 2015.

Mostafavi, Mohsen, Gareth Doherty, and Harvard University Graduate School of Design. *Ecological Urbanism.* Baden: Lars Müller Publishers, 2010.

Mougeot, Luc J. A. *Agropolis: The Social, Political and Environmental Dimensions of Urban Agriculture.* Ottawa: International Development Research Centre, 2005.

Neuhaus, Fabian. *Emergent Spatio-Temporal Dimensions of the City Habitus and Urban Rhythms.* New York: Springer International Publishing, 2015.

Office of Global Analysis, FAS, USDA. *Cuba's Food & Agriculture Situation Report 2008.* (Washington, DC: United States Department of Agriculture, 2008).

Oroza, Ernesto. "Technological Disobedience: Ernesto Oroza." *Assembly Papers.* https://assemblepapers.com.au/2017/04/28/technological-disobedience-ernesto-oroza/ (accessed December 2021).

Ortiz, Fernando. *Cuban Counterpoint, Tobacco and Sugar.* Durham: Duke University Press, 1995.

Peña Díaz, Jorge, and Phil Harris. "Urban Agriculture in Havana: Opportunities for the Future." In *Continuous Productive Urban Landscapes: Designing Urban Agriculture for Sustainable Cities*, edited by André Viljoen, Katrin Bohn and J. Howe. Boston: Architectural Press, 2005.

Pertierra, Anna Cristina. *Cuba: The Struggle for Consumption.* Coconut Creek: Caribbean Studies Press, 2011.

Plan Maestro. "Oficina Del Historiador De La Ciudad De La Habana." www.planmaestro.ohc.cu/.

The Power of Community How Cuba Survived Peak Oil. Directed by Faith Morgan, Eugene Murphy, Megan Quinn and Bruce Corner. Yellow Springs: Green Planet Films, 2006.

Premat, Adriana. *Sowing Change: The Making of Havana's Urban Agriculture.* Nashville: Vanderbilt University Press, 2012.

———. "State Power, Private Plots and the Greening of Havana's Urban Agriculture Movement." *City & Society* 21, no. 1 (2009): 28–57.

Purcell, Mark, and Shannon K. Tyman. "Cultivating Food as a Right to the City." *Local Environment* (2014): 1–16.

Quiroga, Jose. *Cuban Palimpsests.* Minneapolis: University of Minnesota Press, 2005.

Ramirez, R. "State and Civil Society in the Barrios of Havana, Cuba: The Case of Pogolotti." *Environment and Urbanization* 17, no. 1 (2005): 147–170.

Robinson, Jennifer. *Ordinary Cities: Between Modernity and Development.* London: Routledge, 2006.

Rodríguez, Eduardo Luis. *The Havana Guide: Modern Architecture 1925–1965.* New York: Princeton Architectural Press, 2000.

Rosset, Peter, Medea Benjamin, and Global Exchange (Organization). *The Greening of the Revolution: Cuba's Experiment with Organic Agriculture.* Melbourne: Ocean, 1994.

Sant, Alison. "Redefining the Basemap." *Intelligent Agent* 6, no. 2 (2002), Interactive City.

Scarpaci, Joseph L., Roberto Segre, and Mario Coyula. *Havana: Two Faces of the Antillean Metropolis.* Chapel Hill: University of North Carolina Press, 2002.

Sennett, Richard. *Building and Dwelling: Ethics for the City.* Milton Keynes: Penguin Random House, 2018.

Shannon, Lee Dawdy. "'La Comida Mambisa': Food, Farming, and Cuban Identity, 1839–1999." *New West Indian Guide* 76, nos. 1 & 2 (2002): 47–80.

Slow Food International. www.slowfood.com/ (accessed 27 October 2018).

Smith, Neil. "New Globalism, New Urbanism: Gentrification as Global Urban Strategy." *Antipode* 34, no. 3 (2002): 427–450.

Smith, Robin James, and Kevin Hetherington. "Urban Rhythms: Mobilities, Space and Interaction in the Contemporary City." *Sociological Review* 61 (2013): 4–16.

Soja, Edward W. *Postmetropolis: Critical Studies of Cities and Regions.* Malden: Blackwell Publishers, 2000.

———. *Postmodern Geographies: The Reassertion of Space in Critical Social Theory.* Radical Thinkers. London: Verso, 1989.

———. *Thirdspace: Journeys to Los Angeles and Other Real-and-Imagined Places.* Cambridge: Blackwell, 1996.

Spiegel, Jerry, Mariano Bonet, Maricel Garcia, Ana Ibarra, Robert Tate, and Annalee Yassi. "Building Capacity in Central Havana to Sustainably Manage Environmental Health Risk in an Urban Ecosystem." *EcoHealth; Conservation Medicine: Human Health: Ecosystem Sustainability* 1, no. 2 (2004): SU120–SU130.

Staff. "Two Men, the Same Dream." *Granma*, January 26, 2018.

Stanek, Łukasz. *Henri Lefebvre on Space: Architecture, Urban Research, and the Production of Theory.* Minneapolis: University of Minnesota Press, 2011.

———. "Methodologies and Situations of Urban Research: Re-Reading Henri Lefebvre's 'the Production of Space'." *Zeithistorische Forschungen/Studies in Contemporary History* 4 (2007): 461–465.

———. *Urban Revolution Now: Henri Lefebvre in Social Research and Architecture*, Edited by Christian Schmid and Ákos Moravánszky. Burlington: Ashgate Publishing, 2014.

Steel, Carolyn. *Hungry City: How Food Shapes Our Lives*. London: Chatto & Windus, 2008.

Tablada, A., F. De Troyer, B. Blocken, J. Carmeliet, and H. Verschure. "On Natural Ventilation and Thermal Comfort in Compact Urban Environments: The Old Havana Case." *Building and Environment* 44, no. 9 (2009): 1943–1958.

Taylor, Henry Louis. *Inside El Barrio: A Bottom-Up View of Neighborhood Life in Castro's Cuba*. Sterling: Kumarian Press, 2009.

Tiwari, Reena. "Being a Rhythm Analyst in the City of Varanasi." *Urban Forum* 19, no. 3 (2008): 289–306.

Tonkiss, Fran. *Space, the City and Social Theory: Social Relations and Urban Forms*. Cambridge: Polity, 2005.

Turner, John. "Housing as a Verb." In *Freedom to Build: Dweller Control of the Housing Process*, edited by Robert Fichter and John Turner. New York: Macmillan, 1972.

Unfinished Spaces. Directed by Alysa Nahmias, Benjamin Murray and Ajna Films. Oley: Bullfrog Films, 2012.

United Nations Human Settlements Programme. *The Challenge of Slums Global Report on Human Settlements, 2003*. London: Earthscan Publications, 2003.

United States International Trade Commission. *Overview of Cuban Imports of Goods and Services and Effects of U.S. Restrictions*. Washington, DC: United States International Trade Commission, 2016.

Verde Olivo. *Con Nuestros Propios Esfuerzos: Algunas Experiencias Para Enfrentar El Período Especial En Tiempo De Paz*. La Habana: Editora Verde Olivo, 1992.

Viljoen, André, Katrin Bohn, and J. Howe. *Continuous Productive Urban Landscapes: Designing Urban Agriculture for Sustainable Cities*. Boston: Architectural Press, 2005.

Viljoen, André, and J. Howe. "Cuba: Laboratory for Urban Agriculture." In *Continuous Productive Urban Landscapes: Designing Urban Agriculture for Sustainable Cities*, edited by André Viljoen, Katrin Bohn and J. Howe. Boston: Architectural Press, 2005.

Waldheim, Charles. "Notes towards a History of Agrarian Urbanism." In *Bracket 1: On Farming—Almanac 1*, edited by Mason White and Maya Przybylski, 18–24. Barcelona: Actar, 2010.

White, Mason, and Maya Przybylski, eds. *Bracket 1: On Farming—Almanac 1*. Barcelona: Actar, 2010.

Whitefield, Mimi. "Study: Cubans Don't Make Much, But It's More Than State Salaries Indicate." *Miami Herald*, July 12, 2016.

Whyte, William H. *The Social Life of Small Urban Spaces*. Washington, DC: Conservation Foundation, 1980.

Williamson, Rebecca. "Walking in the Multicultural City: The Production of Suburban Street Life in Sydney." In *Walking in Cities: Quotidian Mobility as Urban*

Theory, Method, and Practice, edited by Evrick Brown and Timothy Shortell. Philadelphia: Temple University Press, 2016.

Wilson, Marisa L. *Everyday Moral Economies: Food, Politics and Scale in Cuba.* Chichester: Wiley Blackwell, 2014.

Wirth, Louis. "Urbanism as a Way of Life." *American Journal of Sociology* 44, no. 1 (1938): 1–24.

Wood, Denis. *Rethinking the Power of Maps*, Edited by John Fels and John Krygier. New York: Guilford Press, 2010.

Wood, Lebbeus. "Walls of Change." https://lebbeuswoods.wordpress.com/2010/05/28/walls-of-change/ (accessed October 2015).

Wright, Julia. *Sustainable Agriculture and Food Security in an Era of Oil Scarcity: Lessons from Cuba.* London: Earthscan, 2009.

Wunderlich, Filipa. "Place-Temporality and Rhythmicity: A New Aesthetic and Methodological Foundation for Urban Design Theory and Practice." In *Explorations in Urban Design: An Urban Design Research Primer*, edited by Mathew Carmona. Farnham: Ashgate, 2014.

Wunderlich, Filipa, E. Näripea, V. Sarapik, and J. Tomberg. "Symphonies of Urban Places: Urban Rhythms as Traces of Time in Space: A Study of 'Urban Rhythms'." *Studies in Environmental Aesthetics and Semiotics* 6 (2008): 91–111.

Zakrison, Tanya L., Davel Milian Valdés, and James M. Shultz. "The Medical, Public Health, and Emergency Response to the Impact of 2017 Hurricane Irma in Cuba." *Disaster Medicine and Public Health Preparedness* 14, no. 1 (2020): 10–17.

Index